Graham.
Stewart.

7 Breamar Ave.

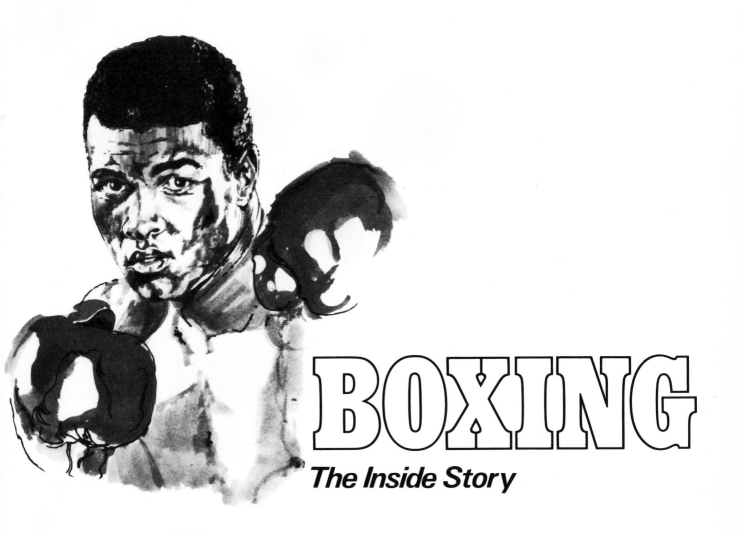

BOXING
The Inside Story

by Gilbert Odd
with a Foreword by **Alexander Elliot,**
Chairman of the British Boxing Board of Control

Hamlyn
London · New York · Sydney · Toronto

Foreword

by Alexander Elliot, Chairman of the British Boxing Board of Control

Over the years, hundreds of books have been published about Boxing, Boxing champions and Boxing in general. To my knowledge, this is the first book which not only relates the early beginnings of the Sport 300 years ago, but proceeds to set out so clearly and in such detail what actually happens behind the scenes in the Boxing world of today.

Boxing is one of the most popular sports screened on Television, and there must be countless thousands of interested viewers who have never actually visited a Boxing Promotion and who may have little knowledge as to what really goes on inside and outside the Boxing ring. In this book Gilbert Odd provides all the answers.

Boxing has often attracted its full share of vocal opponents, but as an Administrator for nearly forty years I am particularly gratified that the author here places on record the numerous strict controls and medical safeguards which the Board have introduced since its inception.

Boxing will never die; the eternal fascination of a duel between two strong men has been fundamental since man began. Under present strict controls, it provides a sport where skill and stamina and courage are all combined. I would only wish that local authorities and schools throughout the land would do more to encourage the young to learn the rudiments of the Noble Art so that youthful energies are channelled into a manly sport, instead of seeking release, unrestrained, in the streets or on the football terraces.

Gilbert Odd is our leading Boxing historian. A Sport deserves the writers it gets, just as a country, they say, deserves the Governments it gets. In this Boxing is very fortunate and I wish this unique and informative book the success it truly merits.

In featuring the champions, the famous personalities and contents, we are aware that perhaps our choice may differ from that of the reader. Yet it must be emphasised that all the names and events are, in the opinion of the author, the editor and the publisher the best selection with which to emphasise *The Inside Story of Boxing*. Some represent the past, others the present and a few symbolise the future.

Contents

HOW IT ALL BEGAN   **6**
The evolution of Boxing from the bare-knuckle days to the modern ring. The famous prize fighters from 1719 to 1892.

THE BOXER   **18**
What makes a boy want to fight. The lure of the ring. The incentives. The unpaid apprentice. Boxing equipment. The weight divisions. The blows in Boxing. The great ones.

THE MANAGER   **38**
The role of the manager. Finding his boxers. Safeguarding their interests. His routine duties. Making the best matches for his men. What he does on the day of a contest.

TRAINING   **52**
Inside the gymnasium. The equipment. The training schedule. The routine exercises. The trainer's role. The duties of the seconds.

THE CONTEST   **68**
The dressing-room. The ring. In the corner. At the ringside. In the ring. The Referee's duties. How to score a contest. The fouls in Boxing. The care of a boxer. The Boxing Sensations.

THE PROMOTER   **94**
The organisation. Conjuring up box-office attractions. The frustrations. A promoter's obligations. The promoter/boxer contract. Famous promoters.

THE AUTHORITIES   **104**
Boxing Commissions and Boards of Control. The way they work and their responsibilities. The legality or otherwise of boxing. Controversial decisions. The scandals. Rags to riches and back.

THE MEDIA   **114**
The history of the Boxing press from broadsheets to sporting newspapers. The filming of fights, radio broadcasts, the vast impact of television on Boxing.

CHRONOLOGY   **124**
The important historic events in Boxing.

INDEX   **126**

First published in 1978 by
The Hamlyn Publishing Group Ltd.,
Astronaut House, Feltham, Middlesex, England.

 © Editor Books Ltd.,
25 Hurst Way, Croydon, Surrey, England.

ISBN 0 600 31458 8

General Editor: William Luscombe

Art & Design: Bryan Austin Associates Ltd.

Typesetting: Tadd Graphics (Typesetters) Ltd.

Colour and Black & White Reproduction: Norwood Litho Plates Ltd.

Printed and Bound in Great Britain: Waterlow (Dunstable) Ltd.

HOW IT ALL BEGAN

The beauty of Boxing is its un-predictability. Champions can be defeated in sensational fashion, favourites come unstuck, knockouts occur out of the blue, referees render debatable decisions, a cut eye can turn probable victory into sudden defeat, a foul blow can earn disqualification when least expected. To bet on a boxer can be as disastrous as wagering on a racehorse. There are no foregone conclusions in the Fight Game. Anything can happen and usually does. The fans can leave an arena after a disappointing show vowing never to go near a ring again, yet the announcement of a contest that has 'natural' written all over it, and back they swarm because of the magnetic attraction that uncertainty brings.

Of course, this is applicable to most sports, but none in quite so fascinating a manner that Boxing provides. If the match is between men of equal weight, skill and experience, it can result in a classic and spell-binding affair, but the best combination from the spectator's viewpoint is a contest between a scientific boxer and a rugged and hard-hitting fighter, with one exploiting strategic art and the other the big punch. Such action makes the crowds roar with excitement with the promoter looking on happily, especially if it is being televised.

Self-preservation being the first law of nature, it is not surprising that man used his fists in defence when no other weapon was at hand. It was also natural that he should develop this basic instinct into a science, also that he would spar with others, not only for the fun of it, but also to increase his proficiency in the art. Spectators of such exhibitions, and especially when a grudge was settled by means of fisticuffs, found it exciting and so the news that two men were to engage in a fist fight or a boxing match, would be certain of attracting a crowd of onlookers. Thus Boxing became a public spectacle which it has remained ever

Above: Ancient Greek Boxing as depicted on a vase in the British Museum. The fingers and wrists appear to be bandaged.

Below: Three forms of the Caestus as worn by Roman pugilists.

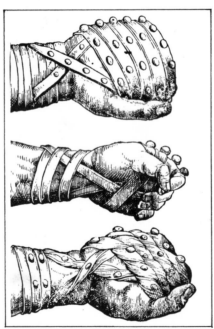

since, its acceptance as a sport coming as early as the original Olympic Games.

The word to describe this form of exercise was Pugilism, from the Greek *pugme* through the Latin *Pugilatus* (the art of fighting with the fists) as also *pugnus*, a fight. The participant became a Pugilist. The term Boxing came from the clenching of the fist, the fingers

turned into the palm of the hand, the thumb laid along the finger nails to form a box, the Greek *puxos*, the Latin *buxus*, in English, a box, although to *box the ears* is usually interpreted as a slap, rather than a blow. The Romans adopted fist fighting in the open-air arenas as one of the circus events, but they went a stage further by permitting the combatants to wear a Cæstus, either in the form of an iron glove, or brass knuckles to slip over the hand. These produced brutal battles that usually resulted in the death of one of the antagonists.

Both among the Greeks and Romans the practice of pugilism, although differing in its main features from our modern and less dangerous contests, was considered essential in the education of their youth, from its manifest utility in strengthening the body, dissipating all fear, and infusing a manly courage into the system. The power of absorbing punishment, however, rather than the art of self defence, seems to have been the main object of the ancients, and he who dealt the heaviest blow, without regard to protecting his own person, stood foremost in the ranks of heroes. Both Homer in the *Iliad* and Virgil in *Aeneid* make numerous references to fist-fighting.

It is understandable how Boxing as a sport and spectacle spread from Athens and Rome to the rest of Europe and to Britain. It formed one of the features of the travelling fairs that towns and villages relied upon for entertainment, and it was particularly welcome in a country where the people have an inborn love of fair play. The British would never tolerate the Cæstus, but they loved a stand-up fight, so the more pugilistically inclined were encouraged to make it a profession, and those who delighted in a display of fist fighting were always ready to back their fancy against a worthy opponent. There were also those ready to promote a battle between two well-matched boxers and to put up a purse containing

Travelling Boxing Booths have been the nurseries for many champions and also, alas, the refuge for old-timers.

gold coins to be awarded to the winner.

Generally, however, the visiting fairs included a boxing booth containing professional pugilists of varying sizes who would invite the public to come and see exhibitions of the Noble Art of Self Defence or to challenge any of the boxing troupe to combat, usually to a decisive finish. Sometimes a town or village would produce its own fistic hero whom they would support to oppose the champion of another place, or to take on any visiting professional.

If there did not happen to be a booth, where entrance money could be taken, those in the pugilistic profession would form a ring, with the onlookers holding a circle of rope. Then one of their number would toss his hat (or castor, the slang name for a beaver hat) into the ring and challenge anyone among the spectators to do likewise. Thus a match was made and if a worthy fight ensued, the onlookers were prevailed upon to throw money into the ring and thus show their appreciation. Usually such donations were presented to the winner, or the men might share by prior arrangement, with the loser taking the lesser amount. The first accounts of prize fighting in Britain come from the 17th century and although only the hands were used, throwing was permitted and it was a most brutal form of entertainment usually ending when one of the contestants was carried unconscious from the ring. It was not uncommon for men of means to make matches between their servants and tradesmen and in the *Protestant Mercury* of January 1681 there is the following report: 'Yesterday, a match of Boxing was performed before His Grace the Duke of Albermarle,

between the Duke's footman and a butcher. The latter won the prize, as he had done many before, being accounted, though but a little man, the best at that exercise in England.' From this it is obvious that Prize Fights were not uncommon events prior to this earliest known journalistic account.

From the early Greek days, a pugilist stood left foot foremost, his left arm being extended, both as a defensive weapon to ward off the blows of an antagonist and as a leading striking force to score points and take an opponent out of his stride, to soften him up for a more damaging blow from the right hand. In Fencing the right hand holds the weapon and the right foot is foremost, this stance being used to keep the heart furthest away from the opponent; in Boxing the left hand is used as a means of defending the heart.

In the days of the Prize Ring blows were permitted to be struck at any part

HOW IT ALL BEGAN

of a rival's anatomy above the belt-line. Wrestling was also allowed, either by a cross-buttock, using the hip as a lever, or by picking up a rival around the waist and throwing him to the ground. The immediate action was then to fall as heavily as possible upon the man after downing him in this way. A round ended as soon as one man had been knocked or thrown down. There was no limit to the number of rounds and the man who was finally left standing was declared the winner. It was deemed foul to strike a man when he was down, to seize him below the waist, to attempt to throttle him or bang his head on the ground when down. Bets were made on such hazards as the first knockdown, first blood, in addition to the actual result.

Just as 'The Turf' became the name for Horse Racing, so 'The Prize Ring' was the term for Boxing. In its early days bare-knuckle fighting took place out-of-doors and a 'ring' was formed by driving stakes into a rough square, then running one, two or even three strands of rope from stake to stake to encircle the combatants. The boxers, with their seconds, one of whom was a bottle-holder, occupied facing corners and no other persons were allowed in the roped square during the contest. There was an outer ring, about a yard in depth, that was reserved for the referee, the umpires (one for each man) the timekeepers (one for each man) the backers, and a few privileged patrons of 'The Fancy'. These were usually the nobility, the young bloods who styled themselves Corinthians, wealthy land-owners and notable men in varying walks of life. In the outer ring also were the Whips, tough men armed with whips whose duty it was to keep the spectators from interfering with the fighters.

A line drawn across the ring, usually with a pointed stick and at the start of each round the men had to come up to this line. If they were too spent to do this they were not 'up to scratch', did not feel 'up to the mark'. If they had made a challenge and then regretted it, they still had to 'toe the line' or meet their obligations. If they were forced into the angle of the ropes that joined

Top left: Boxing contest between natives in Hawaii, such as Captain Cook might have encouraged in his South Seas voyages of the 18th century.

Left: Dutch fisticuffs from an engraving dated 1674.

The business card used by James Figg (or Fig) and drawn for him by the celebrated artist, William Hogarth. Figg (1695-1734) is generally accepted as the first Champion of England in the Noble Art of Self Defence. Oxford Road is now Oxford Street and the site of his amphitheatre was at the juncture with Tottenham Court Road. His cards were distributed at the numerable London fairs and pleasure grounds where he exhibited his physical skills.

Will.   Hogarth f.

James Figg

Master of y Noble Science of Defence
on y right hand in Oxford Road
near Adam & Eve court. teaches Gentle-
-men y use of y small. backsword. &
Quarterstaff. at home & abroad

HOW IT ALL BEGAN

a post, they were 'cornered'. If a man was dropped, his seconds would endeavour to revive him in the 30 seconds allowed for his restoration. If by that time he could not continue then he was deemed to be 'out' of time from which has come the term 'knockout'. The timekeeper would call out when the rest interval had ended, but subsequently, when the crowds became bigger, and there was more noise, a bell was introduced.

These outdoor battles would bring hundreds of followers by all manners of transport, and were natural assemblies for swindlers, thieves and killers, indeed the dregs of the underworld, and during the 19th century disturbances, both before and after a contest, were common. This induced the Law of the time to regard Prize Fights as breaches of the peace and it was the

duty of the local sheriff and his force to break up such gatherings and arrest the chief persons involved, the fighters, the officials and anyone who was not smart enough to get away. To escape the interferences and consequences of the law, it was necessary sometimes to start a 'decoy' fight some distance from the real thing, to try to keep the rendezvous secret, or to choose a site on county borders to make certain of a simple getaway.

The first outstanding Prize Ring personality of whom there is any substantial record, was James Fig (or Figg) (1695-1734), a native of Thame in Oxfordshire, who was more an exponent of cudgels and back-sword play than he was of fist fighting, although he was adept in this direction also. He toured the countryside and town fairs to set up his booth and at Southwark

Fair attracted the attention of William Hogarth, the celebrated artist, who drew a business card for him when Fig, having made a name for himself, opened an academy in 1719 in Tottenham Court Road, London, calling it 'Fig's Amphitheatre'. Here were given displays of all kinds of competitive sport and where he taught the arts of attack and defence to gentlemen. It proved a great attraction, but a year later he moved into Oxford Road (now Oxford Street) where he set up an academy to teach foil-play, backsword, cudgelling, boxing and all the manly arts.

Fig's place in Tottenham Court Road, London was taken over by his pupil George Taylor, who ran it on similar lines and had, as one of his more distinguished patrons, Frederick, Prince of Wales, the father of George

Left: Rules of the Prize Ring drawn up by John Broughton in 1743; the first written rules of Boxing.
Below: A contemporary drawing of Broughton (1704-1789).
Top right: Frederick, Prince of Wales, son of George II, who backed George Stevenson.
Bottom right: William, Duke of Cumberland, Frederick's younger brother, who supported Broughton.

III. In 1723, by order of H.M. George I, a 'Ring' was formed in Hyde Park, London, encircled by a fence for the purpose of staging impromptu conflicts, especially among the 'chairmen' and 'linkmen' of the period. It remained a place of public entertainment until 1820 when it was obliterated by the Bow Street police.

One of the most promising performers at both Fig's and Taylor's establishment was John Broughton (1704-1789) born near Cirencester, who came to London and became a Thames waterman. Standing 5ft 11in and weighing around 14st, he was powerfully built and had a natural aptitude for boxing. After he had defeated the Duke of Cumberland in a fencing match, the royal prince lent him £300 which went towards opening an establishment of his own in Oxford

Road, behind the site of Fig's amphitheatre, and there Broughton was highly successful. This incurred the jealousy of Taylor, who endeavoured to find someone capable of beating the champion. He produced Tom Pipes and George Gretting, both of whom were defeated.

Then George Stevenson, from Yorkshire, challenged Broughton. It was the match of the day. The Prince of Wales backed Stevenson, his younger brother, the Duke of Cumberland, wagered on Broughton. The fight lasted 35 minutes by which time the Yorkshireman was knocked down and out by a fearful blow under the heart. He died several days later and the incident so upset Broughton that in 1743 he drew up a set of Rules for the Prize Ring that were framed in an effort to prevent any such mishap in the future. Broughton's Rules remained in force for nearly a hundred years and they form the basis of all subsequent rules up to the present day.

Broughton's downfall came at the hands of Jack Slack, of Bristol, who landed heavy blows between the champion's eyes to render him blind, then brought him to the boards with a mighty right to the jaw. "What are you about, Broughton?" cried the Duke who had backed the champion to the tune of £50,000. "I cannot see, my Lord", answered the Champion, "Stand me before my opponent and I will fight on". But it was all over in 14 minutes and the Duke was so disgusted at his loss that he declared that he had been 'sold' and renounced Broughton, even having his establishment closed by order of the Legislature, and the beaten man never fought again.

He turned his theatre into a furniture market, bought and sold antiques and curios, speculated successfully on the Stock Exchange and left the sum of £7,000. He made peace with the Duke of Cumberland, who got him appointed a Yeoman of the Guard. He died at the age of 85 and was buried in Lambeth, but a commemorative stone to him exists in the floor of Westminster Abbey. Broughton was also responsible for the introduction of the 'mufflers' the forerunners of the modern gloves which were designed to protect his aristocratic patrons from suffering facial disfigurement.

Slack reigned for ten years before being beaten in 1760 by William Stevens, known as 'The Nailer'. But thereafter the Prize Ring fell into disrepute owing to the boxers accepting bribes and fights being fixed. The nobility withdrew its patronage and devoted its time to horse racing which was becoming increasingly popular, even though the first Derby was some twenty years away. It was Tom Johnson, (1750-1797) from Derby, who restored confidence in the sport by his fistic ability and straight-forwardness. His most historic battle was with Isaac Perrins, from Birmingham, who at 17st outweighed the champion by 3st.

It took place at Banbury and lasted 75 minutes and they fought for £250 a-side with Johnson the winner. Johnson eventually lost the title to Big Ben Brain, from Bristol, who stood 6ft 4in and weighed 16st 6lb Brain retired without defending his championship and on the scene came Daniel Mendoza, an Aldgate Jew (1764-1836) who, apart from being a scientific boxer, became a teacher and even wrote his 'Memoirs'. Mendoza was one of the first to realise how Prize Fighting could be commercialised and during his career he helped promote his own fights, issued tickets, and took money on the door.

His great rival was Richard Humphreys, styled the Gentleman Boxer because he came from well-educated parents. They had three meetings, the first of which, at Odiham in Hants, Humphreys won after 29 minutes whereupon he sent a note to his backer: "Sir, I have done the Jew, and am in good health", while a black pigeon was released by Mendoza's followers which told his East End friends the sad news that they had lost over £50,000 in wagers.

Mendoza gained double revenge, beating Humphreys at Stilton, famous for its cheeses, in 52 minutes and at Doncaster in 65 minutes. Their last fight took place in the yard of the *Rose & Crown Inn* that backed on to the River Don. Tickets were priced at ten shillings, but such was the demand to see the contest that touts were able to secure as much as £10 from clamorous latecomers. After twice defeating Bill Warr, of Bristol, Mendoza claimed the championship of England.

Mendoza's reign came to an end in 1795 when at Hornchurch he was challenged by John Jackson (1769-1845). Because of his stylish dress, his aristocratic bearing and his ability to hold conversation with the best, he was known as 'Gentleman' Jackson, but did not live up to this description when

HOW IT ALL BEGAN

fighting Mendoza as in the ninth round he seized hold of the Jew's long locks and pulled him into several vicious right hand punches until the champion collapsed unconscious.

Jackson did not defend his title, but opened an academy for the teaching of boxing at No. 13 Old Bond Street where, among his many notable patrons, were the Dukes of York and Clarence, 'Old Q' the Duke of Queensberry (ancestor of the famous Marquess) and Lord Byron, whose interest in Boxing was such that he made a screen entirely covered with drawings of famous pugilists of the day and accounts of notable contests.

Jackson formed the Pugilistic Club and when in 1814 the Emperor of Russia and the King of Prussia were entertained in London following the defeat of Napoleon, it was Jackson who was engaged to arrange a fistic evening at the home of Lord Lowther in Pall Mall. Also, at the coronation of George IV, Jackson was asked to provide a bodyguard of 18 prominent pugilists to keep order at Westminster Abbey, because it was feared that those who favoured Queen Caroline, who was not permitted to be present, might cause a riot. All went well, however, and the boxers were rewarded with a letter of thanks and a gold medal between them. This they raffled and it was won by Tom Belcher, of Bristol. Jackson remained a prominent London figure until his death at the age of 76. He was buried at Brompton Cemetery where a

magnificent monument stands to his memory.

During Jackson's lifetime the championship passed into the hands of Jem Belcher, (1781-1811) another native of Bristol, who came to London at the age of 18 and won a number of notable victories, including three in succession over Joe Berks, of Woolwich. Unfortunately, while playing rackets, Belcher lost an eye which caused his retirement. Henry Pearce (1777-1809), another Bristolian, beat Berks and claimed the championship, whereupon Belcher came out of retirement and fought Pearce but was beaten in 18 rounds. Pearce, named 'The Game Chicken' because his friends abbreviated his name to Hen, was a remarkably fine and speedy boxer, who finding it difficult to get opponents went to the King's Bench Prison and sought out a fellow-townsman, John Gully (1783-1863) who had got himself incarcerated there for a small debt of his father's. Pearce proposed that he would secure Gully's release on the understanding that they would fight for the championship.

Gully agreed, the debt was met, and he fought Pearce at Hailsham in Sussex. As a boxer of very limited experience it is not surprising that Gully was beaten, but the fight went 64 rounds and lasted an hour and 17 minutes. Pearce then beat the one-eyed Belcher and retired through ill-health, whereupon Gully twice beat Bob Gregson and claimed the champion-

ship. Gully never fought again, but made considerable money on the race-course and in 1846 won both the Derby and the Oaks with his horses Pyrrus 1st and Mendicant. He became a coal mine owner and was twice returned Member of Parliament for Pontefract.

Another notable pugilist of the period was Dan Donnelly (1788-1820) Champion of Ireland. His greatest victory was over George Cooper in 1815. They met on the Curragh of Kildare and thousands of people left Dublin to see the fight. There is a monument on the Curragh to commemorate the event and Donnelly's footprints to and from the arena have been preserved. The Prince Regent thought so highly of the Irishman that he is alleged to have knighted him with a walking stick at a race meeting, and all subsequent references style him as Sir Dan. A jingle of the time reads:

*"Our worthy Regent was so delighted
With the great valour he did evince,
That Dan was cited, aye, and invited,
To come and be-knighted by his own
    Prince."*

Next on the scene as champion was Tom Cribb (1781-1848), who hailed from the village of Hanham, about five miles from Bristol. A wharfsman, he came into fame by twice beating Belcher, the second time on Epsom Downs, and for winning over Gregson and a black American named Bill Richmond. His name is best remembered, however, for his two exciting battles with Tom Molyneaux, a Virginian slave, brought to London by Richmond. These were the first international matches of any note and aroused tremendous interest. In the first, at Copthall Common near East Grinstead in 1810, the negro had the best of it and continually put the Englishman down.

In the 28th round Cribb could not answer time and Molyneaux was about to be named as the winner, when one of Cribb's seconds ran over to the negro and accused him of carrying bullets in his fists which had wrought such havoc on Cribb. This was denied, but the time occupied over the dispute allowed the Englishman to regain consciousness and resume the contest. A cold rain commenced which caused the black man to shiver and lose confidence and

DANIEL MENDOZA & RICHARD HUMPHREYS

This Boxing Match took place at Doncaster Sep.r 29.d 1790 on a Twenty four foot Stage and was the third Public Contest between these two pugilists. It lasted for about an hour & five Minutes and was decisive in favour of Mendoza —

Mendoza (left) *v.* Humphreys engaged in three contests – Odiham 1788, Stilton 1789 and Doncaster 1790, Mendoza winning on the last two occasions.

12

further misfortune befell him when he threw Cribb heavily and pitched over his body to strike his head against one of the stakes. He was very dazed when he came up for the 33rd round and fell from weakness, whereupon the fight was awarded to Cribb.

Their second meeting was at Thistleton Gap, at a point where the three counties of Leicester, Lincoln and Rutland meet, a convenient escape point in the event of legal interruption. This time the bout lasted only twenty minutes, with both men taking heavy punishment, until a right from Cribb broke the negro's jaw and he was forced to give in, being carried from the arena in a senseless state. Cribb took the Union Arms in Panton Street, off the Haymarket, in London, and here set up a sporting parlour which was patronised by celebrities in all walks of life. When he died a magnificent monument was erected to his memory in Woolwich Cemetery, consisting of a British lion grieving over the dead hero. It was cut from a solid block of Portland stone and weighed 20 tons.

Next on the pugilistic scene was Tom Spring (1795-1851) a native of Hereford. His real name was Thomas Winter and in order to hide his identity when he was introduced to London by Cribb, he changed it to a brighter season. He was a handsome youth, who excelled in graceful boxing of a scientific nature. Of his twelve contests, spread over ten years, he lost only one, to Ned Painter, whom he had already beaten, his defeat being largely due to a severe eye wound he sustained in the first round. Even so he battled on into the 42nd round before giving in.

After Spring had beaten Tom Oliver in 1821, Cribb retired and handed the championship belt to his protégé. Spring twice defeated Jack Langan, the first time in January, 1824 at Worcester Racecourse which lasted 77 rounds, whilst the second, at Warwick five months later went 76 rounds. Spring too, was provided with a majestic monument over his grave in Norwood Cemetery.

Next of importance was Jem Ward (1800-1884), eldest of seven children of a Bow tradesman. Because he worked as a coal heaver in his youth he became known as the 'Black Diamond'. A clever boxer and hard hitter, he won the majority of his contests, but double-crossed his backers in a match with Bill Abbott, by going down in the 22nd round, for which he was paid £100.

Thomas Molineaux, former American slave, who fought many times in England.

Tom Cribb (1781-1848) was undisputed Champion of England for a number of years.

He publicly repented and was allowed to continue fighting and in 1825, after beating Tom Cannon in 10 rounds was acclaimed Champion of England. He lost the title to Peter Crawley, who renounced it a week later, whereupon Ward reclaimed the Championship and made two successful defences. He retired at 31 and took up painting, at which he was a natural adept, and was also a devotee of music. He became a not very successful publican and ended his days in the Licensed Victuallers' Home in the Old Kent Road.

The next man to make his mark in the Prize Ring was James Burke (1809-1845), known as the 'Deaf 'un', because he was born deaf. Burke could neither read nor write and developed into a knuckle fighter when working as a waterman on the Thames. He fought some tremendously long battles, one with Simon Byrne in 1833 lasting three hours 16 minutes and going into the 99th round when Byrne collapsed and died three days later. Burke fled to America where he fought Samuel O'Rourke at New Orleans, and was winning when thugs broke into the ring and the Londoner had to run for his life. He returned to England to fight Bendigo, who claimed the championship, and lost on a foul through butting his opponent in the 10th round.

When a lightweight named Bill Phelps, who fought Brighton Bill, died after being defeated by Owen Swift in March 1838, the rules were re-framed and became known as the London Prize Ring Rules which were adopted all over the world, the principle change

being that no longer were seconds permitted to carry their man to the scratch line at the start of a round, but that he would have to 'toe the line' unaided.

Perhaps one of the greatest of the Prize Ring heroes was William Thompson, known as 'Bendigo', one of triplets nicknamed Shadrach, Meshach and Abednego. Born in Nottingham, he was taught to fight by his mother, who could hold her own against any man. Bendigo was an accomplished boxer, yet five of his most important contests ended in fouls. He claimed the title after beating Big Ben Caunt at Nottingham in 1835, lost on a foul to Caunt three years later, but re-won the championship when Caunt was disqualified in 1845.

He enraged Burke into defeat by his acrobatic antics. His career came to an end when he was showing off by turning a somersault and dislocated his knee. After being imprisoned 28 times for causing a breach of the law, he became a Methodist preacher. Meeting Lord Longford one day Bendigo told him he was now fighting the devil. "Is that so," said his Lordship. "Well, I hope you will treat him a little more fairly than you did poor Ben Caunt." After Bendigo's death a massive memorial was erected to his memory in Nottingham.

Undoubtedly the contest that first attracted world interest in Boxing was between Tom Sayers (1826-1865), a Brighton bricklayer, who had assumed the championship of England by virtue of his successes, and John C. Heenan,

HOW IT ALL BEGAN

claimant to the American title. They met at Farnborough in Hampshire on April 17, 1860, and the fight aroused tremendous national excitement, *The Times* printing a special edition to give detailed coverage to the event, while a Staffordshire Pottery piece was modelled of the two men and had substantial sales. It was the first major international contest since the battles between Cribb and Molyneaux and among the 12,000 that gathered to see it were members of Parliament (including Lord Palmerston) and the cream of the artistic, literary, dramatic and musical worlds.

At 6ft 2in Heenan had an advantage of 5½in and at 13st 13lb was the heavier by 3st. He attacked very strongly, while Sayers defended and countered well, but had the misfortune to have his right arm broken in the sixth round. This was a severe handicap, but he fought on valiantly until the 42nd round when Heenan, who had become partially blinded and was in danger of defeat, seized the Englishman by the throat and bending him over the ropes almost throttled him. At this juncture the police appeared on the scene, the

ropes were cut by one of the spectators and the whole affair ended in a deplorable brawl, the official verdict being a 'draw'.

Sayers never fought again, but Heenan stayed in this country and met Tom King (1835-1888) at Wadhurst in Sussex, but was beaten after 24 rounds. King, formerly in the Royal Navy, had twice fought Jem Mace (1831-1910) for the championship, losing the first battle after 43 rounds, but winning the second in 21 rounds. King retired after beating Heenan, became famous as an oarsman and made a fortune on the racecourse.

To Mace goes the distinction of being responsible for the advance of Boxing as a reputable sport. Born at Beeston, Norwich, he not only was a scientific exponent of the Art of Self Defence but had the ability to teach it. Although only a middleweight (he never scaled more than 11st 6lb) he became heavyweight champion by beating Sam Hurst, known as 'The Stalybridge Infant' who weighed 16st 10lb and stood 6ft 2½in. He lasted only eight rounds against Mace, who then beat off the challenge of Tom King,

The historic Sayers (left) *v.* Heenan international contest fought at Farnborough, England, on April 17 1860 and ending in a 'draw' after 42 rounds lasting 2hrs. 20mins.

who outweighed him by a stone, but lost a return match ten months later. Mace was well ahead until the 19th round when King landed a tremendous right to the head that so dazed the champion that two rounds later his seconds threw in the sponge.

After King's retirement, Mace reclaimed the title and defended it successfully three times against Joe Goss from Wolverhampton. In 1870 he went to America and defeated Tom Allen, a Birmingham man, who had emigrated to the United States. Subsequently Mace had two battles with Joe Coburn, an Irishman who had settled in America, and was then recognised as World Champion. He went to New Zealand and Australia, where he taught boxing and promoted competitions for novices, among his pupils being Bob Fitzsimmons and Peter Jackson. It is significant that Mace introduced his methods throughout the world and is regarded as The Father of Scientific Boxing. He returned to England and, loving to roam, toured the countryside with his boxing booth until he was in his 70's. In 1890, at the age of 59 he met Charlie Mitchell at Glasgow in a contest billed as for the Championship of England. The men wore 6oz gloves and this event led to the end of bare-knuckle fighting in England.

Charles Watson Mitchell (1861-1918) came from Birmingham and was a born fighter, being credited with a fifty minute win over Bob Cunningham soon after his 16th birthday. Although only a middleweight, he won a heavyweight competition in London in 1882 and soon after went to America where he had the temerity to take on John L. Sullivan (1858-1918), who claimed the championship of the world in succession to Mace. Mitchell floored his bigger opponent in the first round, but was so roughly treated afterwards that the police stopped the contest in the third.

Mitchell continued to fight with great success in the United States, but returned to Europe and in 1888 again met Sullivan in a bare-knuckle fight that took place in pouring rain on Baron Rothschild's estate at Chantilly in France. The American tried his hardest to knock out the little Englishman, but Mitchell was too smart for him and was still there in the 39th round when a corps of gendarmes broke up the fight and arrested the contestants. Sullivan paid bail to avoid imprisonment, but Mitchell kept his

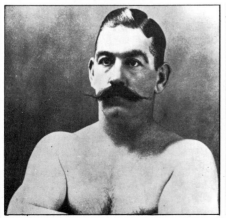

Above: John L. Sullivan (right) claimant to the world's heavyweight title, *v.* Charlie Mitchell, Champion of England, at Chantilly in France, March 10 1888. It lasted 39 rounds and 3hrs. 10mins. 55secs. and ended in a 'draw' with the arrival of a force of gendarmes who arrested the contestants.

Far left: John Lawrence Sullivan (1858-1918) from Boston, Mass.

Left: Charlie Watson Mitchell (1861-1918) from Birmingham, England.

HOW IT ALL BEGAN

money and stayed the night in jail. The contest was declared to have been drawn.

Mitchell then had his glove contest with Mace and in 1894, at the age of 33, returned to America and challenged James J. Corbett for the championship, but was knocked out in the third round. Like Mace and Sullivan, Mitchell was a connecting link between the bare-knuckle era and the wearing of gloves. All three saw the end of boxing under London Prize Ring Rules in 1865 when the 8th Marquess of Queensberry, John Sholto Douglas, in collaboration with John Graham Chambers, a fellow Cambridge student, drew up his famous code that was confined to boxing with gloves.

The Queensberry Rules cut out all the brutality of the Prize Ring, barred wrestling and throwing, made the rounds of limited duration with a minute's interval between them, required the seconds to leave the ring before the start of each round, and gave sole power to the referee, all amendments that improved Boxing as a sport and raised it considerably from the degrading spectacle it had been in the past.

Among the many Englishmen who emigrated to the United States in the early part of the 19th century were several members of the boxing fraternity. Their influence caused the growth of the sport there and by 1816 Jacob Hyer emerged as the first American champion. His son, Tom, gained public and press acclaim in 1841 and after that Prize Fighting continued to flourish and reached a national peak on the emergence of Sullivan.

Known as the Boston Strong Boy, he was no great boxer, but possessed enormous strength and punch power. He claimed the world's championship after beating Paddy Ryan in 1882 and for the next seven years defeated all challengers. He was a national idol and toured Europe, appearing before the Prince of Wales (later Edward VII) at St. James's Barracks, London.

In 1889 Sullivan fought Jake Kilrain at Richburg, Miss. for 10,000 dollars a-side and the championship of the world. Sullivan won in the 75th round after two hours 16 minutes, when Kilrain was too exhausted to fight any further. Immediately afterwards the champion declared that he would never again fight with bare fists and this brought finally to an end the Prize Ring era.

Sullivan's eventual defeat by James J. Corbett in 1892 was the first fight for the Heavyweight Championship of the World under Marquess of Queensberry Rules, therefore the first in which the contestants wore gloves. Sullivan was knocked out in the 21st round and the Richest Prize in Sport has remained in American keeping, except for Bob Fitzsimmons (England) 1897-9, Tommy Burns (Canada) 1906-1908, Max Schmeling (Germany) 1930-2, Primo Carnera (Italy) 1933-4 and Ingemar Johansson (Sweden) 1959-60.

The arrival of Jem Mace, Champion of England, in 1870 did much to improve American boxing as, besides being a talented performer in the classic style, he also proved a great tutor. The adoption of gloves for the Sullivan v. Corbett fight in 1892 virtually saw the end of the Prize Ring. It must also be reckoned that Boxing of some sort or the other was practiced in America from the time of the Mayflower, as all the early American fighters were born in the British Isles.

For a very long time Boxing in America was very much in the hands of unimpeded promoters, large and small, until the State Athletic Commissions, with Boxing Departments, were set up to control the sport because it was getting out of hand, causing public disturbances – even riots.

In New York State the Horton Law controlled Boxing from 1896 to 1900. This permitted fights to be staged without any limit as to the number of rounds, to allow decisions to be ren- dered by referees and for the men to fight for purses and side-stakes. The Frawley Law, 1901-1918 confined the staging of boxing tournaments to membership clubs only and barred referees from giving verdicts, the contests being limited to 10 rounds. This was the 'no-decision' bout era which was favoured in most of the States and was a bad thing for Boxing. In 1920 Mayor Jimmy Walker of New York passed a law permitting referees to give

Max Schmeling

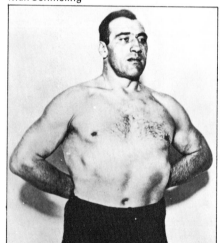
Primo Carnera

Ingemar Johansson

The 8th Marquess of Queensberry

The earliest Champions of America are listed as:

Prize Ring

Class	Champion	Year
Heavyweight	Jacob Hyer	1816
Middle	Tom Chandler	1867
Welter	Paddy Duffy	1880
Light	John McMoneghan	1855
Feather	John Keating	1860's
Bantam	Charley Lynch	1856

Gloves

Class	Champion	Year
Heavy	Jim Corbett	1892
Middle	Jack Dempsey	1884
Welter	Billy Smith	1892
Light	Jack McAuliffe	1884
Feather	Billy Murphy	1889
Bantam	Tommy Kelly	1887

The light-heavy and flyweight classes came at much later dates

decisions, the control of Boxing being in the hands of a specially set-up Boxing Commission. This was followed in most of the remaining States. Up to the coming of television every city and town in the USA had its local promoter, in fact, Boxing proved a major form of sporting entertainment along with Baseball and American Football, and over-riding all else when a major title fight came about. Each place of importance had its boxing arena and the baseball parks and stadiums were taken over for the staging of big outdoor tournaments. Tex Rickard built a huge arena at Jersey City to stage the Dempsey v. Carpentier contest and Mike Jacobs built a large Bowl on Long Island for his major fights.

In addition each town had its own boxing gymnasium – in the cities there were more than one – and these provided the nurseries for the bigger places. The small arenas were the breeding ground for champions. Amateurs were encouraged by the clergy in youth clubs, the police force took boys off the streets and first offenders into their own athletic clubs and the armed forces also encouraged the sport.

Because of the vastness of the country, its many big cities, large entertainment-seeking population and wealth, the United States of America had practically a monopoly of world titles for the first half of the century, but since then the winning of championships have been widespread among other nations, especially with the addition of in-

between weight divisions and the doubling of titles because of competitive controlling bodies. The coming of moving pictures, then radio broadcasts further exploited Boxing, while the televising of bouts to all parts of the world has brought the sport stupefying exploitation.

Millions of people now watch Boxing in their own homes in addition to those enthusiasts who fill the arenas in every country where professional boxing exists. It is principally for this vast new worldwide audience that this book has been written; to provide the armchair fan with the inside information he needs to more thoroughly appreciate this colourful and exciting sport that has crept into their lives. Now for the first time they can be aware of what goes on behind the scenes; that there is far more to Boxing than the entry of the gladiators into the ring; that behind each fighter there are many other personalities upon whom he depends for his status as a paid or unpaid public entertainer. From the fair-grounds of Old England the sport has developed into a highly commercialised business, yet it still demands the utmost in nerve and sinew from its participants if they are to make the grade and become Kings of the Ring.

There was no Prize Fighting in any country in Europe, except when contests were taken there to avoid the law in England. There are two outstanding examples: John L. Sullivan (USA) v. Charlie Mitchell (England) at Chantilly, France in 1888 and Frank

Slavin (Australia) v. Jem Smith (England) at Bruges in 1889. Bare knuckle fighting took place in America from the time the first Englishman landed there.

France: *La Savate*, in which the feet were used as well as the hands, can be traced as far back as 1854, but glove-fighting, known as *La Boxe Anglaise*, did not begin there until 1900. Both British and American boxers helped to develop the sport in France and *La Savate* died out. France became supreme among European countries with such notables as Georges Carpentier, Eugene Criqui and Charles Ledoux. After World War II France produced stars like Marcel Cerdan, Charles Humez and Robert Cohen.

Italy: Boxing began in 1909, again being encouraged by visiting British and American fighters. Many notable boxers were brought to light, including, of course, Primo Carnera. Following the last war Italian boxers have made a great impact on European titles.

Germany: Boxing was taught in Germany long before the turn of the century, but the police authorities were bitterly opposed to it. The first public programme took place at Hamburg in 1899, but it was suppressed thereafter until the ending of World War I. English boxers were then engaged as instructors and the interest in boxing became nationwide, culminating in the arrival of Max Schmeling. Today professional boxing is confined to West Germany, there being none in any country behind the Iron Curtain.

Belgium: Boxing began here in 1910 and many excellent boxers were produced up to World War I. The sport declined from 1946 and was banned for a time, but has since been re-started, although there has always been amateur boxers.

Spain: Pro boxing did not start until after World War I but progressed rapidly, being encouraged by both Britain and France. Many notable fighters were produced, Paolino Uzcudun, being the most prominent, fighting both Joe Louis and Primo Carnera. Since World War II Spain has had a big say in the winning of European titles.

Holland: The Dutch Federation was formed in 1911. **Denmark**, 1889, **Norway** and **Sweden** in 1920, **Finland** 1935, **Switzerland** about the same time. All these countries have produced outstanding boxers from time to time.

THE BOXER

No man has ever been forced to climb into a boxing ring and put up his fists in combat. Thousands have done so since the first recorded bout of 1681 in England, where it all began, but all of their own free will. The enemies of Boxing should remember this when they endeavour to have it banned. And it is not solely for lucrative gain that men are eager to fight, for there are just as many, if not more, amateurs willing to risk a broken nose or a blackened eye for the sheer joy they get from swapping punches.

It must be that most primitive of human urges that makes men want to pit themselves one against the other and strive for supremacy in fistic battle. No doubt it is the first of all our instincts, that of self-preservation. Almost any man will use his hands under duress, but how is it that so many boys delight in the sport of Boxing, for sport it is despite what anyone might say to the contrary, and go on to make a profession of it.

The role of the Boxer has varied with the passing of time. From the Greek and Roman Games, to the notorious Prize Ring days of bare-knuckles bruising in the 17th, 18th and most part of the 19th centuries, to glove-fighting under Marquess of Queensberry Rules. Through the hungry-fighter years of the industrial revolution; the equally submissive days of depression in the 1920's and 30's, and on to the affluent era provided by the vast money to be earned through the medium of film, radio and television rights.

At the outset, both amateurs and professionals are not drawn into the ring because of the lure of medals or money. They are fascinated from early youth with a desire to enter into competition with their fists, both in attack and defence. The reasons are manifold. Firstly, there is family influence. Perhaps a father, brother, uncle or cousin has been or is still a noted boxer. They set an example that becomes an inspiration.

To instance a few cases. There was Brian London, who, like his father, Jack, became British heavyweight champion, while Jim (Spider) Kelly, won the British featherweight title in 1938, then influenced his son, Billy, to do likewise seven years later. There have been numerous fathers who, after a mediocre fighting career, have reared sons who have become champions, one outstanding example being the two Johnsons from Manayunk in Pennsylvania, America. Phil, the father, was no more than a club fighter, yet his son, Harold, became world light-heavyweight titleholder. Yet, strange to relate, both were beaten by Jersey Joe Walcott – Phil in 1936 in three rounds, and Harold in the same number of rounds in 1950. Walcott himself had six children, two of them boys, and although he became heavyweight champion of the world, neither of his sons ventured into a boxing ring. Two renowned British boxers, popular Bombardier Billy Wells and that famous flyweight, Jimmy Wilde, had sons who became professional boxers but did not get very far. Bob Fitzsimmons, Junior, son of the redoubtable Fighting Blacksmith, did compile a useful record as a light-heavy, but never quite got into the championship class.

There have been whole families of fighting brothers – the Turpins, from Leamington Spa, Dick, Randolph and Jackie; the Buxtons, from Watford, Alex, Laurie, Allan and Joe; the Sands from Australia, Dave, Clem, Ritchie, George, Alfie and Russell; the Toweels from South Africa, Frazer, Jimmy, Victor and Willie; the Marchants from Manchester, Jack, Billy, Teddy, Albert, Mark and Matthew; the Famechons from France, Andre, Ray, Emile, Arsenne and Alfred, Andre's son, Johnny, becoming world featherweight champion in 1969; and the Five Fighting Zivics, from Pittsburgh, Jack, Pete, Joe, Eddie and Fritzie, the last-named being the only one to reach championship status.

Dick and Randy Turpin both became titleholders, as did Brian and Cliff Curvis, Harry and Dick Corbett, Chris and Kevin Finnegan. There have been cases where older brothers have gained greater success than a younger and vice-versa. Again there are twins in Boxing, notable cases being the Coopers from Bellingham, Henry and Jim (real name George), while in America there were Mike and Jack Sullivan, from Cambridge, Massachussetts.

THE BOXER
Boxers and their Idols

Many youngsters are drawn into the Fight Game because of a boyhood hero of the ring. Joe Louis, the great Brown Bomber, inspired the equally renowned Sugar Ray Robinson, who delighted in walking home with the future heavy-weight champion and carrying his bag after a training work-out. This was in Detroit, when Louis was 20 and Robinson only 14.

Max Schmeling looked upon Dempsey as his boyhood hero and even managed to break through the Champion's guard during a one round exhibition bout which made Dempsey take note of the young audacious German.

Jack Dempsey was also Freddie Mills' idol and the Bournemouth boy, who had a milk round, would let his float run down any street incline on its own while he ran behind shadow-boxing, in his mind being the famous Manassa Mauler and knocking them out left, right and centre.

Bob Fitzsimmons, the only British-born boxer to win three world titles, including the heavyweight, was Len Harvey's inspiration. Both came from Cornwall and although the latter did not emulate his predecessor in a world sense, he did win British crowns at the identical weights, middle, light-heavy and heavy.

Some boxers have taken up ring careers because of environment; the support of a widowed mother, as in the case of Barney Ross, of Chicago, whose father was murdered by hold-up men in his grocery store, or like Terry McGovern and Benny Lynch, in defence of a street corner newspaper pitch. Again, men like Tommy Farr and Jimmy Wilde, chose Boxing as a more glamorous and lucrative way of earning a living than by working at the coal face in a Welsh mine. But whatever the inducement, there was always the basic, inborn urge, to indulge in fist fighting.

Gene Tunney, whose parents were comfortably off, had no need to box other than to satisfy an inner craving.

His amateur activities were smiled upon, but when he intimated that he would like to turn professional, strong family objections were raised. These he quelled by saying that punches from amateurs hurt quite as much as those from professionals, so why should he come to harm. "If you are born to box – you box".

There have been notable boxers who have adopted the names of famous ring men as an added incentive to their natural urge and aptitude for the sport. Jack Dempsey's real first names were William Harrison, but before him there had been a memorable middleweight champion named Jack Dempsey, whom the fight fraternity called 'The Nonpareil'. There were three American fighters known as Young Corbett after celebrated 'Gentleman Jim', the first heavyweight champion of the world under Queensberry Rules. They were George Green, William Rothwell and Ralph Capabianca Giordano, the latter two becoming world champions at feather and welterweight. The Corbett Brothers from Bethnal Green, adopted the surname in reverence to the same James J., their true name being Coleman. Scottish-born Harry Owens thought the name of a renowned bare-fist fighter, Jake Kilrain, as sounding more formidable than his own, adopted it and won a British championship.

In the past boxers have adopted a *nom du ring* because their own name was not considered to have a fighting sound about it or was too much of a mouthful for the average announcer. Jack Sharkey, heavyweight champion 1932-3, was of Lithuanian descent, his real name being Joseph Paul Zukauskas. Stanilaus Kiecal, changed his to Stanley Ketchel and made it famous as a knockout specialist. Nowadays, with boxers coming from all over the world, the custom of changing a

name to something considered more traditional to the boxing arena has died out and Mexican, Japanese, South American and European proper names are not changed.

There are many more instances of ambitious boxers assuming the ring names of heroes of the past, but others have made the change for other reasons. Jock McAvoy, real name Joseph Bamford, did this to prevent his mother from knowing that he was boxing professionally at Royton Stadium in Lancashire on a Sunday afternoon. Another, for the same reason was Pontypridd-born Frederick Hall Thomas, who ultimately became light-weight champion of the world as Freddie Welsh.

THE BOXER
Born to be a Boxer

Only those with an unquenchable urge to put on the gloves ever venture into a boxing class at school or into a gymnasium afterwards. Most preparatory schools, public schools and the Universities have facilities for any boy who is boxing-minded, while the Services encourage the formation of a boxing squad, many good ring warriors emanating from the Army, Navy and Air Force as was seen following the two world wars. If a school has a games master who is interested in Boxing, then any pupil who shows desire and promise gets the encouragement he needs, even if he does no more than box as an amateur and for the sheer fun of it.

Boxers are born, not made. It takes great courage to come from a corner to test one's skill against that of another and only a dedicated boxer can do it. There has to be that impelling desire to swap punches before a boxing career in its very earliest stages can be contemplated; a welling-up of that instinctive urge to fight with nature's weapons.

In addition to all the inner impulses and yearnings, there must be the mind and matter to go with them. Physical toughness is essential, plus the frame on which to build muscular development, both to absorb the shock and pain of taking punches and to achieve retaliative hitting power and ringcraft. Nervous strength is another vital asset; the ability to keep calm under pressure and to remain cool and collected when victory seems in sight. All the ambition and desire in the world will not produce a worthwhile boxer if the physical and mental requisites are not there basically.

In this connection it is obvious that apart from the arduous business of actual fighting, a boxer is called upon to wear gloves weighing either six or eight ounces and to carry this weight on each hand for upwards of an hour can be very demanding of a person who is not at the peak of physical fitness.

One other quality urges a boy to seek

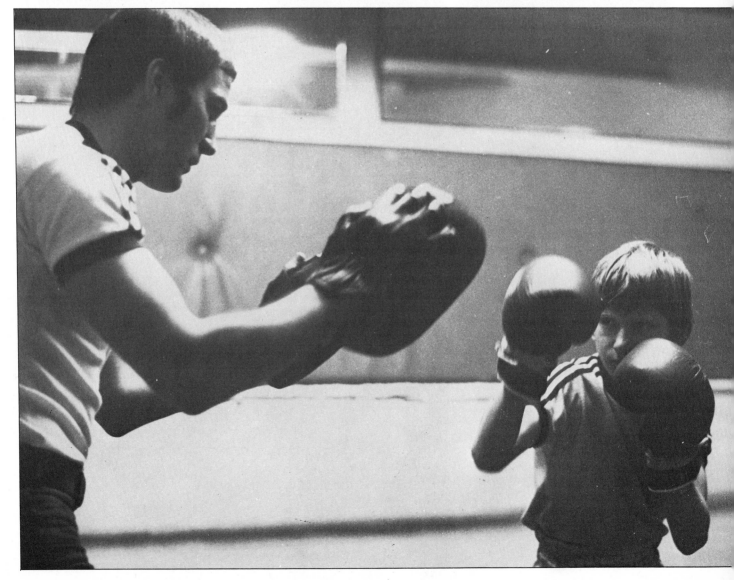

THE BOXER

stardom in the ring – the thrill of performing before an audience and the public adulation that comes to those who reach fame. Even during training sessions in the gymnasium there are always onlookers, attracted to the sport even if not physically equipped to participate. There are well-wishers and friends far exceeding in number those enjoyed by the average youngster. There are advisers and wouldbe instructors on all sides and a young boxer has to discriminate between the real and the unreal, the genuine helpers and the mere hangers-on.

Though training for Boxing is hard and arduous, to the dedicated boy it is thoroughly enjoyable in all its aspects, even the roadwork that would seem deadly dull and unproductive to the average person is undertaken with dogged zeal because its unquestionable value is fully appreciated, while the satisfying feeling of supreme physical fitness is worth all the concentration and will-power demanded.

Of course, the shadow-boxing and the sparring with other boxers provides the more exciting parts of the training routine, again because the enjoyment of the actual work is implemented by the presence of onlookers. The successful fighter is an entertainer at heart, with the added incentive of the prizes, money and glory to be won. Even in the bare confines of a gymnasium he can fantisise that it is the real thing, that he is in there facing someone equally determined to win a battle of wits, skill and strength, egged on in his endeavours by the natural desire to be victorious, plus the electrifying atmosphere created by the greedy fans, intent on extracting the utmost in satisfaction for their money.

Unpaid Apprenticeships

It is obvious that all boxers must emerge from the amateur ranks and usually this means joining a club at an early age and under skilful guidance pass through the various stages, first as a novice, then into competitions and, if progress is sustained, eventually to become a class boxer in specialised bouts. In the unpaid class the wheat is sifted from the chaff and those who fail to make the grade have to be content with watching and aiding those more talented and better equipped than themselves for the rigorous life of a glove fighter. From such unsuccessful amateurs come the club administrators, the trainers and the keen supporters.

Amateurs may not have monetary awards, at least that is the intention and supposition. But there are medals and cups to be gained, national and international titles to be won, with the ultimate ambition to earn 'gold' at the Olympic Games. Such distinction is an automatic passport into the professional ranks and many of the great champions of the world, such as Floyd Patterson, Muhammad Ali (as Cassius Clay), Joe Frazier, George Foreman, Nino Benvenuti, Pascual Perez and Frankie Genaro, all were final winners at the Olympics and went on to win world championships as professionals.

In Great Britain, the Amateur Boxing Association rules the unpaid

side of the sport, with its Annual Championships. There are also the Commonwealth Championships held every four years, which produce a high standard of amateur efficiency. Most Continental countries have similar institutions and there are the European Championships held every two years, the winners of which are assured of welcome into the paid ranks if they feel so inclined. The institutions include:

Federazione Pugilistica, Foro Italico, Rome
Federation Francaise de Boxe, 62 Rue Nollet, Paris
Royale Federation Belge de Boxe, 15 Avenue Defre, Bruxelles
Federation Suisse de Boxe, Case Postale, Basle 2
Federation Espagnole de Boxe, Montera 44, Madrid
Federation Hellenique de Boxe, 4 Rue Capsali, Athens
Bund Deutscher Berufsboxer, Potsdamer Strasse, Berlin 30
Nederlandes Boksbond, Emmalaan 10, Amsterdam 2
Federation Turque de Boxe, Physique Necatibey Caddesi, Ankara
Svenska Boxingsforbundet, Sveavagen 29, Stockholm
Osterreichischer Berufs Box Verband, An den Hulben, Vienna 1.

Right: Gold For Cassius Clay. Olympic Games 1960. Light-heavyweight medal line-up.

Opposite page:
Top: Swift transit. Charlie Magri (right) winning his 1977 A.B.A. flyweight title. Within seven months he became British champion in his third paid fight.

Bottom left: Smokin' Marvis , Joe Frazier's son (right) winning a Golden Gloves contest in Philadelphia.

Bottom right: Gold Strike. Joe Frazier wearing the Olympic Games gold medal he won at Tokyo in 1964. Six years later he was world's heavyweight champion.

In America each State has its own amateur controlling body, the main urge for pugilistically inclined young-sters being the famous Golden Gloves tournaments. These cover almost the whole country and there are City, Inter-City, State, Inter-State and finally National titles to be won at all weights. The whole is covered by the Amateur Athletic Union and no boy can compete, or box for that matter, unless he has an A.A.U. card. Whilst every boxer who partakes in amateur bouts is supposedly void of any pay-ment whatsoever, there is remuneration of kind that can be converted into cash. The usual practice to encourage ama-teur talent in the United States is to offer watches to prize winners which can be 'sold back' to the organisers or their representatives after the award has been made.

Amateurs in all parts of the world can receive generous expenses, while in some countries the top boxers are given State employment as an inducement. These methods of getting round the strict amateur code are unfortunate, but quite irrepressible, more especially in countries where the standard of living is comparatively low. In all its history the flow of boxers has come from the under-privileged classes that is why in England, for example, where there were once thousands of fighting men, they have now dwindled to a few hundred.

Not every top-notch amateur pro-ceeds automatically into professiona-lism. Many very talented unpaid performers resist the urgings of their supporters and the tempting offers

THE BOXER

made to take off their vests and step into the ring for money. Managers and their agents are constantly on the watch for class amateurs who can be persuaded into making a livelihood with their fistic abilities. Many resist the temptation, however, for one reason or the other, an outstanding case being that of Eddie Eagan, an American who became captain of the Oxford University boxing team and won a silver medal at the Antwerp Olympic Games in 1920 as a light-heavyweight. He resisted all efforts to get him to become a pro, but did not relinquish his interest in Boxing, later becoming chairman of the New York State Boxing Commission.

Another prime example was Harry Mallin, who was A.B.A. middleweight champion five times from 1919-23, was European champion in 1924 and twice was a gold medallist at the Olympic Games of 1920 and 1924. He would never consider boxing for pay and on retirement devoted his time to the amateur cause in Great Britain. Likewise, his brother Fred was five times an A.B.A. middleweight champion, from 1928-32, and was Commonwealth champion in 1930. He, too, could never be induced into becoming a professional.

The bright lights

More often, however, the lure of the ring, the arc lights, the accepted ceremonies, the roar of the crowd and the general exciting atmosphere proves very attractive to a youngster who has built up a good reputation as an amateur and he discards his Simon Pure status with alacrity, eager to fight his way to the top and earn the wealth and public adulation that comes the way of the successful professional.

Once a young man decides to make a living from Boxing he must first apply for a licence from his controlling body and, unless he has a relative or close friend to guide him correctly, should acquire the services of a reputable manager, one who will look after his interests and who has the right connections so far as promoters are concerned. The boxer will be beholden to his manager in all matters that concern his fighting life, although, if he is wise, he will not hesitate to voice an opinion whenever an important decision is made. He will then fit himself out in a manner appropriate to professionalism, both in bearing and appearance.

Boxing Equipment

The equipment required by a modern boxer is of the simplest. A pair of abbreviated trunks or shorts, a jock strap and protective cup for the genitals for wear underneath; socks, and a pair of regulation boxing boots specially designed to protect the ankles from being turned over and laced high above the instep. Those, his bandaged hands and his gloves are all that he takes into the ring with him, although he comes from the dressing-room wearing a wide-sleeved dressing robe to keep him warm whilst waiting for the bell when a rubber gum-shield is popped into his mouth by his chief second.

In his training he needs a track suit, plus extra clothing if he is being called upon to make a specific weight, sweat shirt, leotards, etc. Usually, his gymnasium apparel is additional to that he wears for a contest. He also requires special gloves for ball or bag punching, plus a skipping-rope, although these are items that are available for his use at the training quarters. Some boxers favour the use of head-guards when they are sparring, especially if they are susceptible to cuts or have scar tissue around the eyes that needs protecting. On the other hand, I have known famous boxers disdain the use of head-guards because they hold the view that it makes a man careless and less inclined to the avoidance of punches by adroit movements of the head.

While the majority of top-ranking boxers confine themselves to their profession, many of the lesser lights and up-and-coming boys, if they are wise, have extra forms of employment or careers to which they can return when their fighting days are over. In former days the ex-fighter of any repute would become the licensee or landlord of a public house where he could still command public admiration and respect. But the less fortunate drifted into mediocre employment, usually because, after a lengthy period of life as a boxer, they were not fitted or trained for any more lucrative job.

Boxers of today who have regular work apart from their boxing activities, usually train in the evenings, unless they can get special time off for an important bout when they use the gymnasium in the day-time, which gives them the opportunity to mingle with the full-time pros and perhaps spar with them, or they can pick up tips to improve their own ability. As Terry Downes maintained, if you rub shoulders with the best some of the gold must brush off on to yourself. Some boxers, however, prefer to train in the evenings to coincide with the time they usually go into the ring for an actual contest.

The day of the average top-class, full-time, professional starts early in the morning. If he is living in a town, he is up at 5-30 or 6 a.m. and, clad in his track suit and sweater, he does his roadwork, five, eight or ten miles as required, to put power in his legs, develop his lungs to intensify his breathing, strengthen his heart and build up stamina and physical endurance. He may have another boxer or his trainer to keep him company – trotting alongside or riding a bicycle. Usually the run ends in a 200 yards sprint. He has a bath and rub down, eats a hearty breakfast, then relaxes, perhaps sleeps, until around 11 or 11-30 a.m. when he proceeds to his training quarters.

Here he meets his trainer, or manager – sometimes the two occupations are confined to the same person. They have the boxer's next engagement in mind and plan the session accordingly.

After his work-out, the boxer showers, dresses and then goes off for a substantial lunch, steak if he can get it, avoiding all fatty and fat-making foods, but eating plenty of vegetables and fresh fruit. He then takes a long rest, a two or three hour sleep, after which he has a light tea, then the rest of the day is his own. Usually it finds him back at the gymnasium to watch others at work and to mix with the fight fraternity. He will not miss a boxing show if he can help it, going there, not only to give prospective future opponents a look over, but also to pick up tips from the performances of boxers in a higher class than himself and where he can be introduced from the ring and improve his public image. At public promotions he gets further opportunities to meet other members of his profession in their various catagories.

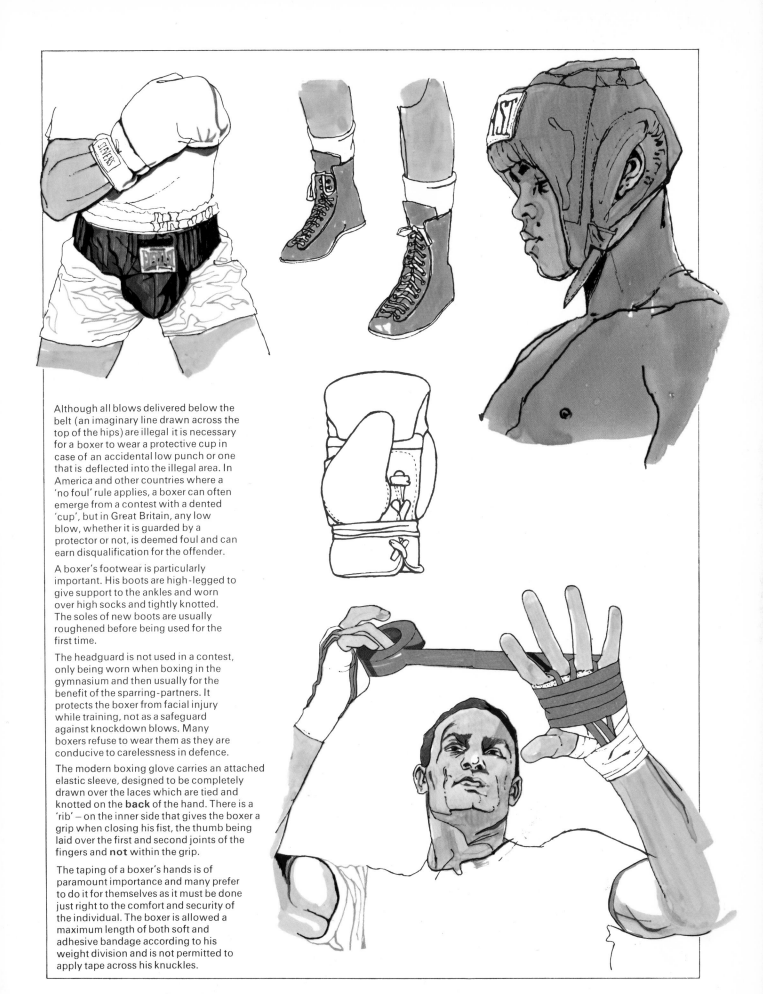

Although all blows delivered below the belt (an imaginary line drawn across the top of the hips) are illegal it is necessary for a boxer to wear a protective cup in case of an accidental low punch or one that is deflected into the illegal area. In America and other countries where a 'no foul' rule applies, a boxer can often emerge from a contest with a dented 'cup', but in Great Britain, any low blow, whether it is guarded by a protector or not, is deemed foul and can earn disqualification for the offender.

A boxer's footwear is particularly important. His boots are high-legged to give support to the ankles and worn over high socks and tightly knotted. The soles of new boots are usually roughened before being used for the first time.

The headguard is not used in a contest, only being worn when boxing in the gymnasium and then usually for the benefit of the sparring-partners. It protects the boxer from facial injury while training, not as a safeguard against knockdown blows. Many boxers refuse to wear them as they are conducive to carelessness in defence.

The modern boxing glove carries an attached elastic sleeve, designed to be completely drawn over the laces which are tied and knotted on the **back** of the hand. There is a 'rib' – on the inner side that gives the boxer a grip when closing his fist, the thumb being laid over the first and second joints of the fingers and **not** within the grip.

The taping of a boxer's hands is of paramount importance and many prefer to do it for themselves as it must be done just right to the comfort and security of the individual. The boxer is allowed a maximum length of both soft and adhesive bandage according to his weight division and is not permitted to apply tape across his knuckles.

THE BOXER
The Weight Divisions

The eight classes at this date were:

Flyweight	...	...	...	up to 8st (112lbs)
Bantamweight	...	...	...	up to 8st 6lb (118lb)
Featherweight	...	...	...	up to 9st (126lb)
Lightweight	...	...	...	up to 9st 9lb (135lb)
Welterweight	...	...	...	up to 10st 7lb (147lb)
Middleweight	...	...	...	up to 11st 6lb (160lb)
Light-heavyweight	...	...	...	up to 12st 7lb (175lb)
Heavyweight	...	...	...	over 12st 7lb

The weight divisions in which a boxer operates is defined by his natural build. As a youngster he may pass through several classes before reaching a poundage at which he remains during his best years as a fighting man. In the early days of Boxing there were only three divisions; light, middle and heavy, so that many men whose natural weight was in between often had to fight at a disadvantage. Later, as the sport became more sophisticated, bantam, feather and welter classes were added and subsequently light-heavy (cruiser in England) and fly-weight classes were added. The first standardisation of weight divisions came in 1909 and were issued by the National Sporting Club, with its head-quarters in Covent Garden, London. With them were introduced Lord Lonsdale Belts which gave authenticity to British championships.

These weights have remained ever since and are standard throughout the world. In between classes have been added from time to time, the first, known as the Junior-Welterweight class being introduced in America in 1922 when there were a number of natural ten-stone (140 lb) men who either had to reduce drastically to compete as lightweights, or had to give away too much weight to genuine welters. Since then other 'Junior' or 'Light' classes have been brought in, not only to make for fewer weight differences between fighting men, but also to create more championship titles to be won, thus giving promoters extra opportunity to stage matches of public appeal.

At the present time the weight divisions have increased to 13 by the addition of the following:

Light-Middleweight	...	...	up to 11st (154lb)
Light-Welterweight	...	...	up to 10st (140lb)
Junior-Lightweight	...	...	up to 9st 4lb (130lb)
Light-Featherweight			
or			
Super Bantamweight	...	...	up to 8st 10lb (122lb)
Light-Flyweight	...	...	up to 7st 10lb (108lb)

The N.S.C. Belts (*top left*) denoted British Championships and were introduced by the National Sporting Club of London on November 8, 1909. They were known as the Lord Lonsdale Challenge Belts, the 5th Earl (*left*), who was President of the famous Club, giving his name to them. They were modified (*left centre*) by the British Boxing Board of Control in 1930. The 'Ring' Belts (*bottom left*) were introduced in 1922 by Nat Fleischer and are presented to every holder of a world championship irrespective of nationality, by the 'Ring Magazine', New York, U.S.A.

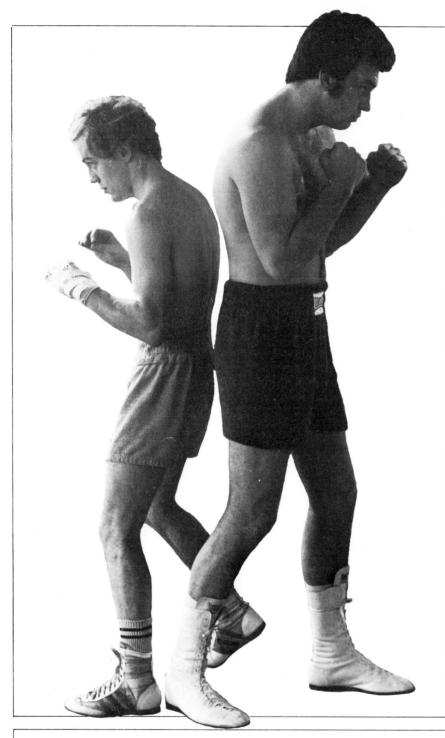

This illustration gives some idea of the general physical difference between featherweights and heavyweights, but of course there are very tall small men just as there are very short heavyweights. Tommy Burns at 5ft 7½ins was the shortest man ever to win the World heavyweight title, while at 5ft 11ins Al Brown of Panama was the tallest bantamweight World champion.

The last two new weight classes were introduced for the benefit of men of small stature, such as the Japanese, Thailanders, Philippinos, etc. In the early days of glove fighting in Britain, boys and men below eight stones in weight usually boxed in an unofficial class known as Paperweight.

Although this is not intended to be a book of instruction, it is appropriate to show the fundamentals of the Art of Self Defence – the punches and the counter-punches and the basic moves that a boxer has to learn until he does the right thing at the right time instinctively. It is also important to try and read the other man's mind, to foresee his intentions and to thwart his plans, but of course, perfection can only be reached by experience. Balance is another prime essential, either when delivering a punch or avoiding one, for to be caught off-balance can be disastrous.

Prior to the Second World War, the boxer who stood side-on, with his left foot advanced, and led with a straight left, was considered to be orthodox. Left-handed, or 'southpaw' boxers as they are known in America, who led with the right from a right foot foremost stance were frowned upon by the purists, even turned round and made to adopt a left foot forward position and lead with the left, as many left-handed school-children were forced to write with their right hands by the majority of teachers in those unenlightened times. Nowadays, the 'southpaw' boxer is accepted and quite a number have become champions. This style makes all their punches and moves exactly opposite to the 'orthodox' boxer. Unless he is a left hook specialist, the orthodox boxer's most potent weapon is his right, whereas with the 'southpaw', it is his left that has to be watched, unless, of course, he is a noted right hook exponent.

The hook, a devastating punch, is a shortened swing and is achieved by turning the wrist sharply on the point of impact. Famous Kid McCoy claims to have invented it after studying the rifling of a gun. He called it the 'corkscrew' punch (see page 30).

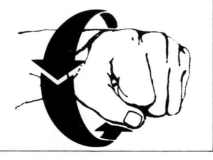

THE BOXER

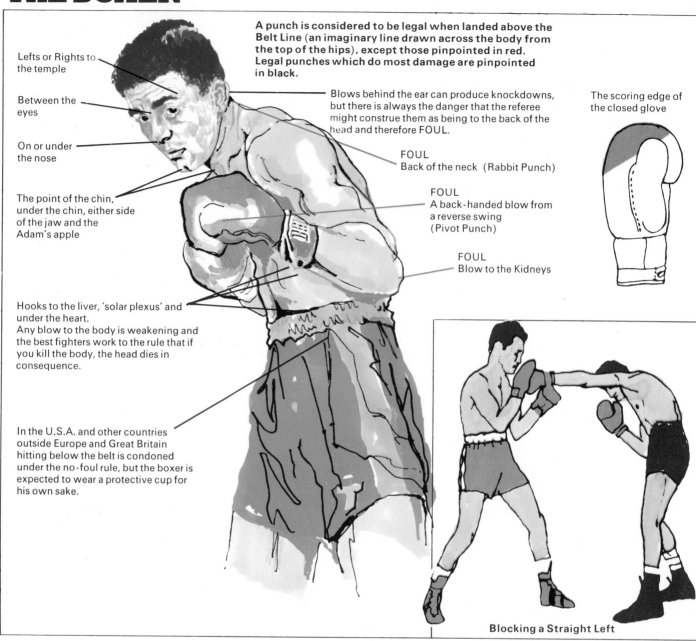

Lefts or Rights to the temple

Between the eyes

On or under the nose

The point of the chin, under the chin, either side of the jaw and the Adam's apple

Hooks to the liver, 'solar plexus' and under the heart.
Any blow to the body is weakening and the best fighters work to the rule that if you kill the body, the head dies in consequence.

In the U.S.A. and other countries outside Europe and Great Britain hitting below the belt is condoned under the no-foul rule, but the boxer is expected to wear a protective cup for his own sake.

A punch is considered to be legal when landed above the Belt Line (an imaginary line drawn across the body from the top of the hips), except those pinpointed in red. Legal punches which do most damage are pinpointed in black.

Blows behind the ear can produce knockdowns, but there is always the danger that the referee might construe them as being to the back of the head and therefore FOUL.

FOUL
Back of the neck (Rabbit Punch)

FOUL
A back-handed blow from a reverse swing (Pivot Punch)

FOUL
Blow to the Kidneys

The scoring edge of the closed glove

Blocking a Straight Left

The Blows in Boxing

Attack is the best form of defence and the best attacking weapon is the straight left lead to the face or body. The boxer holds his left glove high as a defensive guard against a right and shoots it out straight and true to the centre of his opponent's face, the mouth, the nose, or between the eyes. He can move in closer and shorten the blow to a jab, the most popular punch in the modern ring, the policy being to advance behind a stabbing jab that compels the opponent to retreat. Euclid tells us that the shortest distance between two points is the straightest, therefore straight punching is quicker than swinging and more effective as speed is the essence of Boxing.

The left hook, a jab with the wrist turned inwards at the point of impact,

can be a swift and destructive blow when delivered by an expert. This is a blow specially favoured by Henry Cooper and many other famous ringsters and was originated by Kid McCoy, a clever American middleweight. When handling a rifle one day he asked how it had got its name and was told because of the rifling inside the barrel, it being further explained that a bullet travelled faster and truer if it was revolving as it left the gun. The Kid thought the same process might work out as a Boxing move and after trying it out on a punch-bag used it against his next opponent who was knocked cold. McCoy exploited his new punch to build up a great reputation as a potent puncher.

The Straight Left, or left swing or

Continental Stance   American Stance   Right Uppercut to the chin   Left Hook to the side of the face

Right Hook to the face   Right Cross over a Straight Left

left hook to the body have three qualities. They sap a man's stamina and reduce his resistance; they cause him to lower his guard as a protective measure and so expose his chin to a switched punch over his dropped forearm; while if delivered directly and with power to the nerve centre immediately below the ribs in the centre of the body, it can knock all the wind and fight out of a man and put him down for the full count. This punch was originally known as Broughton's Mark, being used with great expertise and efficiency by this early British prize-fighter. When Bob Fitzsimmons used this identical blow to win the heavyweight championship of the world from 'Gentleman' Jim Corbett, it was acclaimed by an American newspaper reporter as the Solar Plexus punch and the name stuck. Other damaging blows to the body are rights under the heart or beneath the rib cage on either side of the body. Punches to the kidneys are deemed foul as are those to the back of the neck or anywhere below the 'belt', an imaginary line drawn across the tops of the hips.

Of course, the main purpose of the straight left is to pave the way for a following straight right, or right hook, to the head. Bewildering an opponent with a series of straight lefts or jabs makes him an easy target for a sizzling right-hander to the jaw that could well end a contest decisively. In fact, the modern boxer uses a good deal of combination punching, switching from one hand to the other and to varying parts of the anatomy in bursts of rapid fire, against which an opponent is forced to retaliate in like measure, clinch or go into retreat.

Counter blows are as important as the leads. The straight right cross counter is delivered over a left lead and is a most effective blow being aimed at the jaw – the most vulnerable part of the human make-up, the point of the chin being the target for scoring a knockdown or knockout. Blows to the head cause the opponent to raise his guard, thus exposing his body and vice versa. Naturally the counter-puncher must be swift in his retaliation and take advantage of every opening he sees. Left foot forward boxers rarely lead with a right, preferring to use it as a

THE BOXER

follow-up to a well-timed left lead. A great match-winning punch and the one that excites the spectators even when it misses, is the upper-cut that comes from left or right and can be driven through a rival's defence either to the midsection or the head. Accurately delivered, the back of the hand facing the target.

The punching methods used by boxers vary according to their individual build and size. A tall man, with a correspondingly long reach, prefers long-range exchanges, while a shorter, more compact man relishes in fighting where he can batter away two-fistedly. Feinting is a great art, aiming a blow but not delivering it and then putting over a punch from an unexpected angle or from the other hand. Success at Boxing largely depends on outwitting an opponent and the art of feinting, or deceiving, is something to be brought to the acme of perfection. In his footwork the boxer uses a gliding movement and has to control his actions, either going forward, retreating or side-stepping. All must be done smoothly and with a cool head, the gloves held high, elbows tucked into the sides, so that his arms and shoulders, plus his gloves, form a defensive barrier, even when on the attack.

Finally, the present day boxer must be mentally alert to all that is going on around him. He may have been born with a natural aptitude for fighting, possess all the physical requirements, be game and courageous, but above all he needs to realise that his boxing career can, at the very most, last only a small proportion of his life; that if he can still make money in the ring up to the age of 30, or a few years more, there is a far longer period of time ahead when his present fistic talents will have little influence on his earning capacities in the future. Should he gain world fame and his name becomes a household word, then he may find lucrative employment because of it, but the great majority of ex-boxers must start afresh to make a livelihood, in all probability in a vastly lower wage rate from the purses he has been in the habit of picking up. It is the wise boxer, therefore, who either saves from his ring earnings for his retirement, by investments or annuities, or has become efficient in a side-line occupation during his boxing days, so that he does not find himself on the scrap-heap when the time comes to take off his gloves for good.

The Great Ones

It is the Giants of the Ring that command most public interest and admiration if only because the bigger they are the harder they fall. All the world's heavyweight champions have had something about them that has made them worthy of winning the Richest Prize in Sport, but some are outstanding and they are listed in chronological order.

HEAVYWEIGHTS

John Lawrence Sullivan from Roxbury, Mass. U.S.A. First claimed the world crown when a barefist fighter after beating Paddy Ryan in 1882 and Jake Kilrain in 1889. He was so tough and destructive they called him The Boston Strong Boy and he has remained America's legendary hero of the Fight Game. Standing 5ft 10in and weighing 190lbs (13st 8lb), he was beaten only once in 75 contests. Kept title for ten years.

James John Corbett. San Francisco, Calif. U.S.A. Known as 'Gentleman Jim' because of his manner of dressing and his ability to mix in the best of society. First heavyweight champion with the gloves under Marquess of Queensberry Rules. Actor as well as brilliant boxer who used science in preference to brute force. Stood 6ft 1in, weighed 184lbs (13st 2lb) and became champion after beating Sullivan in 26 rounds. Stayed as titleholder until 1897.

Bob Fitzsimmons. Helston, Cornwall, the only English-born boxer to win the world title by knocking out Corbett in 14 rounds, a marvellous feat as he never weighed more than 165lbs. (11st 11lbs). Started boxing career in New Zealand and Australia, then went to America where he became world middleweight champion in 1891, heavyweight champion in 1897 and world light-heavyweight champion in 1903 at the age of 40. Height 5ft 11¾ins.

James Jackson Jeffries. Carroll, Ohio, U.S.A. Became champion in his 13th professional bout by knocking out Fitzsimmons in 11 rounds. A powerfully-built man, standing 6ft 2½ins and weighing 220lbs (15st 10lbs) Heavy puncher, he retired undefeated in 1905 after being champion for six years. Was persuaded to come out of retirement in 1910 to fight Jack Johnson but was beaten in 15 rounds.

John Arthur Johnson. Galveston, Texas, U.S.A. Known as Jack Johnson. First black boxer to win heavyweight crown which he did in Sydney, Australia, on Boxing Day 1908 by stopping Tommy Burns in 14 rounds. Made several successful title defences, but ran foul of the law and fled to Europe. Search made for a 'White Hope' capable of beating him, but it was not until 1915, when he was 37 that he lost his crown to Jess Willard. Height 6ft 0¼ins. Weight 195lbs (13st 13lbs).

William Harrison Dempsey, from Manassa, Colo. U.S.A. Boxed as Jack Dempsey and nicknamed The Manassa Mauler because of his savage and destructive manner of fighting. Won title in 1919 by demolishing Jess Willard in three rounds. Fought sensational battle with Luis Angel Firpo, a giant Argentinean, who knocked the champion out of the ring before being put down and out in second round. Lost title to Gene Tunney in 1926. Stood 6ft 0½in and weighed 190lbs (13st 8lbs).

James Joseph Tunney. New York City, N.Y. U.S.A. Boxed as Gene Tunney and came into prominence when winning service championship as a light-heavy in 1919. Known as The Fighting Marine, he was an upstanding stylist making excellent use of a straight left. Won heavyweight title by out-pointing Jack Dempsey over ten rounds in 1926. The following year in a return fight he again outpointed Dempsey, but came close to defeat in the seventh round when he was floored in what has become known as The Battle of the Long Count. Was defeated only once in 76 contests and retired unbeaten for the title.

Maximillian Adolph Siegfried Schmeling. Boxed as Max Schmeling. Named 'The Black Uhlan' in America. Born at Klein Luckow, Brandenburg, Germany, 28.9.1905. Began pro boxing 1924. Won light-heavy and heavy-weight championships of his own country and became European heavy-weight champion before proceeding to America where in 1930 he won the vacant Heavyweight Championship of the World on a foul over Jack Sharkey; the only man in Boxing history ever to win the big title whilst lying on the canvas. Lost title to Sharkey on a disputed points decision a year later. Caused a sensation by being the first man to knock out the hitherto unbeaten Joe Louis, a victory that should have gained Schmeling a chance to win back his world crown. Because of his nation-ality, however, he was denied the opportunity by the machinations of Promoter Mike Jacobs, and when he did eventually meet Louis in a return bout two years later, Max was knocked out in the first round. World War II brought his career to an end.

Primo Carnera. Sequals, Italy. Giant-size, he began working in a circus in his 'teens as a strongman and wrestler, but was encouraged to take up Boxing, being brought to Paris by promoter Jeff Dickson. After six years of pro fighting, involving 81 contests (of which he win all but six) he became world heavyweight champion by knocking out Jack Sharkey in six rounds at Long Island, New York. At 6ft 5¾in he was the second tallest heavyweight champion, being just a half-inch shorter than the giant cowboy Jess Willard. But he was the heaviest at 260 pounds. Carnera made two success-ful defences of his title before losing it to

Max Baer, who floored him eleven times during the 11 rounds it lasted. Subsequently beaten by Joe Louis in six rounds, after which he went down rapidly and finally went back to wrestling with great success. Known as The Man Mountain, Da Preem, Satchel Feet and The Ambling Alp.

Joseph Louis Barrow. Lafayette, Ala, U.S.A. Fought as Joe Louis and nick-named The Brown Bomber. Won world title at the age of 23 by knocking out James J. Braddock in 8 rounds in 1937. Defended title record 25 times, retired undefeated 1949. Attempted comeback the following year but failed to regain championship. Height 6ft 1½in Weight, 200lbs (14st 4lb). Fine upstanding boxer, noted for his left jab and precise punching power that gained him 54 inside-the-distance wins out of 71 bouts.

Tommy Farr. Tonypandy, Wales. Started boxing as a boy-miner and won the Welsh light-heavyweight title at the age of 19. Was unsuccessful in his attempt to win the British title at that weight, but created a surprise when becoming British heavyweight cham-pion by outpointing Ben Foord, of South Africa. Caused astonishment when he defeated Max Baer, former world titleholder, and a sensation

when he knocked out Walter Neusel, of Germany, in three rounds. Gave Joe Louis one of the hardest fights of his career when challenging for the world title in New York in 1937 – the fight all Britain sat up to hear over the radio. Never defended British title owing to outbreak of World War II. Made a remarkable comeback in 1950 at the age of 36 which ended after 16 bouts when he was stopped by Don Cockell who was 14 years younger than Farr.

Rocco Francis Marchegiano, from Brockton, Mass. U.S.A. Fought as Rocky Marciano and won title in 1952 by knocking out Jersey Joe Walcott in 13 rounds. Defended title successfully on six occasions and retired undefeated in any of his 49 contests, all but six of which ended by a knockout or the referee's intervention. Tremendous, non-stop puncher, a human tank. Stood only 5ft 11in and weighed 184lbs (13st). Killed in an air crash in 1969 the day before his 46th birthday.

Floyd Patterson. Waco. N.C. U.S.A. At 21 became youngest boxer ever to win world heavyweight title. Was the first boxer ever to win it twice. In 1952 was Olympic Games middleweight gold medallist. Height 6ft Weight 182lbs (13st). A fast-moving boxer of considerable talent, who lost his title to Sonny Liston under a considerable weight handicap.

Ingemar Johansson. Sweden. Tal-ented amateur who caused consterna-tion among his admirers by being disqualified for 'not trying' in the final of the heavyweight competition in the

THE BOXER

1952 Olympic Games at Helsinki. Turned professional and, after serving in the Swedish Navy, won the European heavyweight title in his 15th paid contest. Noted for his right-hand punch which he named 'The Hand of Thor'. Went to America to score a sensational three rounds victory over Floyd Patterson for the world's championship, putting the titleholder down seven times. Lost title in return bout with Patterson a year later and failed to regain same in a third meeting. Retired unbeaten as European champion at age of 31. Sweden also produced Harry Persson, who became Champion of Europe in the 1920's, but was not quite good enough to challenge for the world crown.

Cassius Clay. Louisville, Ky. U.S.A. Won Gold Medal at 1960 Olympic Games at light-heavyweight. Turned pro 1960, won heavyweight title in 1964. Changed name to Muhammad Ali. Made nine successful defences of his crown, then forfeited title. Regained it in 1974. A skilful boxer who made use of every square inch of the ring. Notorious for his publicity eloquence. Undoubtedly the most colourful boxer of all time.

LIGHT-HEAVYWEIGHTS

Georges Carpentier. Lens. France. Began boxing at the age of 13. Became champion of his own country and of Europe at all weights from welter to heavy. Beat all British heavies of his day and challenged Jack Dempsey for world title in 1921. Won light-heavy world title in 1920 and lost same to Battling Siki, from Senegal, in 1923. Won 51 contests inside the distance, mainly by use of a swift straight right to the jaw.

Battling Siki. Senegal, F.W.A. Real name Louis Phal. Brought to Paris by French actress, but losing her patronage, became a dish-washer in a restaurant. Picked up his boxing when serving with American troops in World War I and won many contests with his wild-swinging punches and ring antics. Created sensation by stopping Georges Carpentier, the Idol of France, to win the world light-heavyweight crown, but lost this to Irish-American Mike McTigue in Dublin on St. Patrick's Day during the Troubles in 1923. Went to America and enjoyed a mixed record before being murdered in a street brawl in 1925 at the age of 28.

Freddie Mills, Bournemouth, England. Began as a booth boxer at the age of 16 and had grown into a light-heavy by the time he was 23. Won British version of world title in 1942 by defeating Len Harvey in two rounds. Added to his claim by defeating the American champion, Gus Lesnevich in 1948. Lost title to Joey Maxim in 1950 after gallant attempt to win British heavyweight title from Bruce Woodcock the year previous.

Archibald Lee Wright. Benoit, Miss. U.S.A. Boxed as Archie Moore, winning the world title at the advanced age of 36, although his mother declared he was three years older. Was never beaten for the light-heavyweight crown which was taken away from him in 1962 when he was fighting heavies, twice making unsuccessful bids for the championship. Fought 228 battles, won 193, 140 of these being inside-the-distance, and earned eight drawn verdicts.

MIDDLEWEIGHTS

Stanislaus Kiecal. Grand Rapids, Mich. U.S.A. Boxed as Stanley Ketchel and because of his hard-hitting and knockout record was known as 'The Michigan Assassin'. Won world title in 1907 at the age of 21. Fought the redoubtable Jack Johnson for the heavyweight crown and succeeded in putting the champion down but was knocked out shortly afterwards. Was undefeated as middleweight champion when he was murdered in 1910.

Edward Henry Greb. Pittsburgh, Pa. U.S.A. Boxed as Harry Greb and fought in such non-stop fashion that he was known as 'The Human Windmill'. Had 290 bouts in a career lasting 13 years and remained champion from 1923 to 1926. Also defeated Gene Tunney for the American light-heavyweight title. Died after operation on eye at the age of 32 while still an active boxer.

Edward Patrick Walker. Elizabeth, N.J. U.S.A. Boxed as Micky Walker and because of his tenacious style of fighting was known as The Toy Bulldog. Was world welterweight champion from 1922 to 1926 and middleweight titleholder from 1926 to 1931. Was paid £20,000 to defend his crown against Tommy Milligan, the British champion, whom he knocked out in ten rounds at Olympia, London.

Walker Smith. Detroit, Mich. U.S.A. Boxed as Sugar Ray Robinson. Won welterweight title in 1946, defended it five times without defeat. Won middleweight championship five times to create a stupendous record. Lost title to Randolph Turpin in London in 1951 and regained it in New York 64 days later. Started boxing at the age of 20 and continued until he was 45. The greatest middleweight of all time.

Marcel Cerdan. Sidi Bel Abbes, Algeria. Rugged, hard-punching youngster, he was unbeaten in Casablanca, becoming French welterweight champion in 1938, a title he never lost. Won French middleweight championship in 1945 and two years later became European titleholder at that weight. In 1948 knocked out Tony Zale in Jersey City to become world champion, but lost championship to Jake La Motta in Detroit nine months later, having to retire with an arm injury after ten rounds. Flying back to America for a return fight, his plane crashed in the Azores and he was killed. In his favourite cafe in Paris there is the chair he used, with no one being allowed to sit on it.

Carlos Monson. Born at Sante Fe in the Argentine on August 7th 1942. After a brilliant amateur career, turned professional at the age of 20. Discovered by Amilca Brusa who managed him from start to finish. Won Argentine middleweight championship in his 40th contest in 1966 and the following year won the South American title. In 1970 he caused a sensation by knocking out Nino Benvenuti for the world middleweight crown in Rome. Made 14 successful defences in the next seven years and retired unbeaten on July 30th 1977 to become a full-time film actor. Had 101 fights of which he won 88 and lost only three, the others being drawn. His hard punching and determined aggression enabled him to score 60 inside-the-distance wins. Undoubtedly to be ranked high among world middleweight champions.

WELTERWEIGHTS

Gershon Mendeloff. St. Georges, London. Boxed as Ted (Kid) Lewis and because of his non-stop style was known as the Dashing, Crashing Kid. Began boxing at 15. Won first championship at 19. Went to America and won welterweight championship of the world by defeating Jack Britton in Boston in 1915. Fought Britton 20 times in next six years with the title changing hands on several occasions. Returned to England to become welter and middleweight champion of Great Britain and Europe.

Barnet Rosofsky. New York, N.Y. U.S.A. Boxed as Barney Ross. Won the lightweight and junior lightweight titles in 1933, then took the welterweight crown from hard-hitting Jimmy McLarnin. Lost it back to McLarnin, but recovered the championship in a rubber match. Made stubborn defence of title against Henry Armstrong in 1938 in memorable battle. Lost only four of 82 professional contests.

Henry Jackson. Columbus, Miss. U.S.A. Boxed as Henry Armstrong, being nicknamed 'Homicide Hank' because of his large number of inside-the-distance wins. Only boxer ever to hold three world championships at one and the same time. Feather October 1937, welter May 1938 and light August 1938. In 175 contests, won 144 (97 on knockouts or stoppages) and fought eight drawn bouts. Fought a 'draw' for the middleweight championship.

LIGHTWEIGHTS

Oscar Nelson. Copenhagen, Denmark. Fought as Battling Nelson and was so tough he was called 'The Durable Dane'. Fought coloured Joe Gans at Goldfield, Nevada, in 1906, in what was the most historic contest between lightweights, ending in Nelson's disqualification in the 42nd round. Won title from Gans two years later and lost it to Ad Wolgast by a knockout in the 40th round in 1910.

THE BOXER

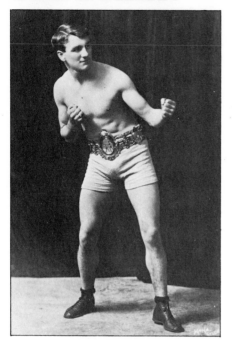

Frederick Hall Thomas. Pontypridd, Wales. Fought as Freddie Welsh. Started professional boxing career in America at age of 19. Came home to win British lightweight title and the first of the Lord Lonsdale Belts. Defeated Willie Ritchie, of America, for the world crown at Olympia, London, 1914 and remained champion until 1917 when he was knocked out in nine rounds by Benny Leonard in New York.

Benjamin Leiner. New York, N.Y. U.S.A. Boxed as Benny Leonard and after winning the title from Welsh at the age of 21 proved himself to be one of the greatest lightweights of all time. An upstanding, scientific boxer he retired as champion in 1925. Became a referee and died in the ring whilst officiating in 1947 aged 51. Of 209 contests was beaten only five times.

Tony Canzoneri. Slidell, La. U.S.A. Because of his speed and great punching power was known as 'Little Pizan'. Started pro fighting at 16. Fought a 'draw' for bantam title in 1927, won featherweight title the following year. Won lightweight crown in 1930 with a one round knockout victory over Al Singer. Won junior-welterweight title from Jack (Kid) Berg. Kept lightweight crown until outpointed by Barney Ross in 1933. Regained championship two years later, but lost it finally to Lou Ambers in 1936. Won 138 of 181 bouts with eleven drawn.

FEATHERWEIGHTS

John Terence McGovern, Johnstown, Pa. U.S.A. Boxed as Terry McGovern and because of his vicious hitting was known as 'Terrible Terry'. Knocked out British champion, Pedlar Palmer, in one round to win world bantam title in 1899 and then became featherweight titleholder the following year by beating George Dixon in eight rounds. Defended crown six times before losing to Young Corbett II who beat him surprisingly by a two rounds kayo in 1901.

Jim Driscoll. Cardiff, Wales. Greatest exponent of scientific boxing ever seen. They called him 'Peerless Jim'. Won British title and first Lonsdale Belt awarded to the division in 1910. Outboxed the world champion Abe Attell, in a non-decision contest. Was never granted a fight for the title. Beaten only twice, the last occasion when he was 38.

William Guiglermo Papaleo. Middletown, Conn. N.Y. Boxed as Willie Pep and because of his fleetness of foot and fast punching was known as 'Willie the Wisp'. Won title in 1942 at the age of 20 and defended against all comers until defeated by Sandy Saddler six years later. In a return fight he regained the championship, and kept it until 1950 when he was again beaten by Saddler. Had 241 contests in 26 years of professional fighting and lost on only 11 occasions.

Joe Saddler. Boston, Mass. U.S.A. Boxed as Sandy Saddler. Tall for a featherweight at 5ft 8½in his long reach enabled him to win 144 of his 162 contests with two drawn. Was still reigning champion when an eye injury in a car crash caused his retirement at the age of 30. Two full years of his career were lost during service in the American Army.

BANTAMWEIGHTS

Alphonse Theo Brown. Panama, C.A. Boxed as Al Brown. Abnormal height of 5ft 11in for a bantam, his long reach served him well in his 25 years in the ring. Won the world title in 1929 at the age of 27 and defended it successfully on nine occasions, mostly in Europe, finally losing to Baltazar Sangchilli in Spain in 1935. Won 123 of his 156 contests, with 12 drawn. Good puncher, especially with uppercuts to the body.

Manuel Ortiz. Corona, Calif. U.S.A. This Mexican-born bantam became world champion in 1942 and kept the title for eight years, losing finally to Vic Toweel in Johannesburg. Defended his championship record 21 times, losing it to Harold Dade in 1947 but regaining it 64 days later. Won 92 of his 122 bouts, 45 inside the scheduled distance.

Robert Cohen. Bone, Algeria. Brilliant, fast-moving bantam with big punch, he became Champion of France in third professional year. Followed this by winning the European title three months later in Belfast, knocking out John Kelly in three rounds in 1954. Gained world crown by defeating Chamrern Songkitrat in Bangkok the same year. Successfully defended championship by boxing a draw with Willie Toweel in South Africa, but lost his laurels to Mario D'Agata of Italy, in Rome in 1956, after which he retired.

Ruben Olivares. Mexico City. Began boxing at the age of 18 and won the world title from Lionel Rose, of Australia, in 1969 by a knockout in five rounds. Stopped in 14 rounds by Chuchu Castillo to lose championship, but regained it from the same boxer six months later. Held bantam crown until 1972. Became world featherweight champion in 1974 and again in 1975.

FLYWEIGHTS

Jimmy Wilde. Tylorstown, Wales. Ex-miner who stood only 5ft 2½in and and weighed 108lb (7st 10lb), yet carried dynamite in his gloves. He was known as The Tylorstown Terror and The Ghost with a Hammer in his Hand. Won British title in 1916 and the same year beat two Americans, Johnny Rosner and the Young Zulu Kid, to secure recognition as world champion. Remained titleholder until 1923 when at the age of 31 he went to America and lost crown to Pancho Villa, nine years his junior.

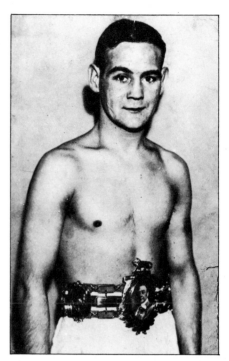

Benny Lynch. Clydesdale, Scotland. Brilliant two-fisted boxer who started at 18 and won the British, European and World titles when knocking out Jackie Brown of Manchester, in two rounds. Fought a sensational battle with Peter Kane, from Golbourne, who was beaten in 13 rounds, then outpointed Small Montana, the American champion, to receive universal recognition as world titleholder. Lost his title on the scales when unable to make the weight in a championship bout.

Jackie Paterson. Springfield, Ayrshire, Scotland. Hard hitting southpaw flyweight who won world title when knocking out Peter Kane in 61 seconds in 1943. Kept title for five years, losing eventually to Rinty Monaghan after experiencing great difficulty in making the flyweight limit. Also became British and European bantamweight champion. Murdered in South Africa in 1966 at the age of 46.

THE MANAGER

To achieve the highest and most satisfying results from his endeavours, the young pro boxer requires the assistance of two essential people – a knowledgeable and conscientious trainer and a competent and business-like manager. Just as authors, artists and actors need the advice and guidance of an agent in order to gain the maximum reward for their efforts, so the aspiring boxer requires a resourceful intermediary between himself and any promoter who may require his services.

The best manager is one of long experience who has the respect of the promoters. It is fatal to appoint as manager a relative or a close friend who will learn the business at the expense of his protege. There is no room for sentimentality in the boxing jungle. The young fighter needs someone to look after his interests, both in and out of the ring, and the appointment of his mentor can make or break him. The choice of the right man must be made with the utmost care.

While family ties are to be commended, the installing of a blood relation as manager can have anything but the best results. There have, of course, been fathers, brothers and other relatives who have steered boys to fame, but in the main it is better for all concerned if a complete outsider is given this important role. There is always the danger that family or parental pride can usurp reality and common-sense to the detriment of the boxer; such as not recognising that he has reached a point where retirement from a contest is the wisest course. This natural, but exaggerated faith in a boy's ability by someone in charge who has the closest ties can bring about over-matching or drastic weight reduction at a crucial point in a promising youngster's career and so bring it to an early curtailment.

Selecting the right manager presents another problem; whether to join up with one who commands a large stable of boxers or the man who can devote the highest proportion of his time to the service of one boxer. Of course, the man with many good boys under his wing commands greater attention from promoters, but if the manager with a single boxer to whom he devotes his entire attention can raise him to championship class or into an outstanding box-office attraction, he will find no difficulty in selling his services.

Another observation to be made before teaming up with a manager is to make sure he does not already have in his stable a prominent boxer in the same weight division as this can easily lead to the more experienced man getting extra attention from the manager and more opportunities to rise in the profession, thus leaving the newcomer in the role of playing second-fiddle. There was the notable case of Alf Mancini, a high-ranking welter from Notting Hill in London, who found himself in the same stable as Jack Hood, a Birmingham stylist, who became champion and then went on to challenge for the middleweight title while still holding the championship for which Mancini was fully qualified to fight. Alf had to wait for years until he was allowed to challenge Hood, who then beat him narrowly on points. It is best in a large stable to be the sole fighter at your personal poundage.

The acquisition of a competent trainer is of equal importance and again there is reason for making a sound choice. The ideal is to have a capable manager who is an equally capable trainer, thereby saving in outlay, at least on paper, but a situation that should not be adopted merely for economic reasons. The manager who confines his attentions solely to the furtherance of his boxer's interests and earning capacity is in some respects the better man to employ. He can select a trainer in whom he has the utmost confidence and leave matters to him, at the same time making sure there is the maximum liason between them. Harmony between boxer, manager and trainer is essential if success is to be achieved, and a vital step if both are in the corner with the boxer for a contest, is to decide who shall be the chief second – the one to whom the boxer turns for advice and who will be solely responsible for his welfare throughout the bout.

The manager who is more concerned with being a publicity agent may produce better financial results, but it is

the trainer who must deliver the fighter in the physical condition to earn the highest monetary rewards. Trainers are usually former boxers who cannot keep away from the Fight Game when their own careers have come to an end. These make the best instructors and conditioners because they have themselves been through the mill, but only if they have the ability to impart their knowledge and experience to the young boxer in their care. Some great champions have proved themselves to be the worst possible trainers or instructors simply because they lack the power to teach or care for others.

Every manager and trainer must be licenced by their controlling body and for simplicity and convenience the rules and regulations of the British Boxing Board of Control* and the way it administers them will be taken as a standard guide, as their procedure varies with little in importance in other countries. Everyone connected with Boxing in Britain in an earning capacity must hold a licence which is issued annually, but a manager is not granted one initially unless he has been registered in another category for at least a year during the previous ten This procedure is to ensure that no person without previous experience in the Boxing set-up is allowed to control the destiny of a youngster who

*In the author's opinion these are the finest and best administered in the world.

THE MANAGER

has shown great promise in the amateur ranks, or as a high-ranking fighter has been lured away from someone else who has brought him to that high peak of earning ability. In any event, every applicant for a licence in any category must appear before the boxing authorities and satisfy them that he is a reliable and capable person to whom the welfare of a boxer can be committed with safety. In Britain a manager's licence costs £12, a matchmaker's £5.

With every boxer under his care a manager must have an official contract, the term of which must not exceed three years when it can be renewed if both parties are willing. If the boxer is under age in a legal sense, the contract must be witnessed by his accredited guardian. In the event of a boxer becoming a champion during the period of the contract the manager has the option of renewing same for a further three years, this being only fair to the

During the days preceeding a contest, the gymnasium is a hive of activity with trainers, managers and seconds involved, as well as the boxers in training for impending contests.

THE MANAGER

Managerial Duties

man who has brought the boxer along from nothing to championship status and safeguards him from losing his protege to another manager who would thus reap the rewards without having lifted a finger in bringing the boy to stardom. This is not an automatic procedure, however, for the boxer has the right to object to the extension of the contract, but must satisfy the Board of Control that he has a good and sufficient reason for so doing.

In Britain managers are not permitted to 'sell' an interest in their boxer's earnings to another person, although this has been a practice in various countries, especially America. Even so the authorities there do their utmost to stamp it out, it having been established that notorious gangsters have 'bought' a large interest in champion boxers and then influenced their ring performances to make betting scoops. Another important B.B.B. of C. rule is to insist that the two parties in a Manager/Boxer contract do not reside more than 50 miles apart for obvious reasons, unless it can be proved that satisfactory arrangements are made for the proper supervision of the boxer's training.

In the contract the manager undertakes to secure contests and/or other avenues whereby the boxer may benefit, such as exhibition bouts; music hall, theatre, film, radio and television appearances; the engagement as a sparring partner to another boxer, also literary contributions to books, magazines, newspapers, etc. that appear under the boxer's name. On his part, the boxer undertakes to accept all engagements secured by his manager and also to keep himself in the fittest possible physical condition to enable him to give of his best in the fulfilment of any work obtained for him by his manager.

When it comes to dividing the earnings of the boxer, the manager is entitled to 10 per cent when the amount does not exceed £30. When the receipts exceed £30, after deducting reasonable training and travelling expenses, including the cost of employing sparring-partners, the manager is entitled to deduct 25 per cent from the net sum as his commission. This percentage is applicable for contests in Great Britain and all European countries, but for fights taking place in other parts of the world, America, Australia, etc., the manager's share is increased to $33\frac{1}{3}$ per cent.

It is the duty of the manager to keep in constant touch with his boxer; to map out a plan of campaign that is mutually agreeable and to console him in the event of defeat, giving constructive criticism and encouragement for the future. He should give sound advice as to how his boxer should conduct himself out of the ring, to appreciate the fact that he is an athlete and must restrain such indulgences as drinking alcohol, smoking, or anything that is considered detrimental to his well-being.

Most managers ban sexual intercourse during training, even when the boxer is married, in fact, the majority do not encourage marriage up to the peak of a fighting man's career, as more often than not a wife's influence can upset the confidence her husband has in his trainer or manager. Some wives have proved great assets to their boxer husbands, others have unwittingly impaired their progress. Len Harvey was lucky with his Florence, Jimmy Wilde owed much to his 'lizbeth, Bob Fitzsimmons' winning of the heavyweight championship has often been attributed to the exhortations of his wife Rose, while Lew Jenkins was glad to have Katie in his corner when he fought his way to the lightweight title. On the other hand, Jack Dempsey met trouble with Estelle and Joe Louis had to part with Marva, while Sugar Ray Robinson's marriage to Edna Mae eventually came to grief.

It is not logical for the average wife fully to appreciate what the life of a fighting man involves, the sacrifices that have to be made and the dedication to his work that is demanded, or to understand the strain he undergoes whilst in strict training. Nor do some of them take kindly to the fact that a large purse paid to her husband is subjected to certain heavy deductions before the balance reaches his hands, or that a manager should receive what she considers too big a percentage of her man's earnings when only one of them is taking the punches. The glamour of marrying a man who has a big public following, the colourful atmosphere of the fight scene, and the delight in sharing the limelight with her husband, are not always complete compensation for the times when she is forced into being a boxer's widow when her man is away from home at a training camp.

On the question of a boxer's earnings there is one thing that I have always advocated, but which has not as yet found its way into the official duties of a manager, i.e. to give advice on the saving of money for the future and insisting on the putting aside part of each purse to cover income tax demands. No matter how brilliant a boxer may be in the ring, it does not follow that he is a master-mind when it comes to finance. In the past I have had ex-boxers come to me for details of their fighting records of years back because they have suddenly received demands for unpaid tax on monies earned and which they have neglected to return to the income tax authorities.

It is natural that the temporary affluent boxer should think more of buying a new flashy car than putting the money aside for tax payments and in my view it should be written into the manager/boxer contract that the first-named should be held responsible for making out his fighter's income tax return. I know of some managers who do this as a matter of course, but it should be regarded officially as a bounden duty. Referring once again to Joe Louis. In spite of having two managers and being under contract to the greatest promoter in the world, he was forced to make a comeback at the age of 37 in order to find the money for his unpaid income tax. This ended disastrously with an eight rounds knock-out defeat by the far younger Rocky Marciano and when he finally hung up his gloves the one-time Brown Bomber still owed the United States Treasury something in the region of a million dollars. For years he was plagued with this debt until, with no hope of it ever being paid, it was wiped off as a gesture to a great public character.

After each contest a manager must make out a detailed written financial statement to his boxer and this would be the ideal time for stressing the importance of preserving some of the purse balance for income tax purposes, even insisting on this being done, or keeping a record himself for the boxer's benefit.

To do full justice to a promising fighter, a manager needs to devote considerable time other than attending his training sessions. He should be right up-to-date in fistic matters on a world scale, even keeping the records and ratings of all boxers whom those in his stable may be called upon to meet. In Britain, if nowhere else in the world, there is a weekly publication* devoted entirely to the sport which has been going since 1909 and from its pages a live manager can keep *au fait* with the current fistic situation wherever Boxing is practiced. There are sources from which other information can be obtained, notably in America where there are a number of periodicals devoted to the Fight Game.

The manager should attend all the boxing promotions he can, especially to watch those who are possible opponents for his own boys at a future date, while at the same time maintaining close contact with all those connected with the sport. He must keep on good terms with everyone, especially the promoters; see that his boxers carry out the engagements he makes for them to the best of their ability; use every form of publicity available to advance their interests by correspondence, use of telephone and personal contact with boxing writers, sports editors, radio and television interviews and the like and also encourage fan mail by having his boxers photographed and give-away cards printed for him to autograph.

The successful manager must be able to assess the purse value of his boxer so that he gets the best possible terms for his services. He should have, or obtain, detailed knowledge of any fighter that is proposed to him as a suitable opponent for his own boxer so that there is no possibility of him being over-matched or made to suffer any disadvantage that might result in him being beaten. This is particularly important when the opponent is a foreigner.

I once heard a manager excuse himself for getting his boxer defeated by stating with indignation that he did not know the other man was a 'south-paw', whose style completely bewildered his own boxer who had never before met a right-foot foremost warrior. Another foolishly admitted that he had not bothered to read the

Boxing News.

contract for the fight and did not realise until it was too late that he had engaged his boxer, not only to fight ten rounds for a sum of money that was only worthy of eight, but of more disgraceful significance, had let his boy train for only eight rounds, this being the extent of his experience to date. Arthur Boggis, a former fighter and subsequently an astute manager of several champions, had one stock question to ask a promoter when being offered an opponent for one of his men. "Has he ever been knocked out?" he would enquire, and if answered in the affirmative, would say unhesitatingly: "He'll do," it being his belief that once a boxer had suffered that indignity, it could always happen again, a factor that gave his own fighter a psychological advantage.

The efficient manager (if he is not also the trainer) never misses a training session in which his boxers are involved. It is his duty to see that they are in, or getting into, prime condition, going through a thorough work-out and, above all, in the right mental approach to a forthcoming contest. On such occasions he has the opportunity of discussing with his men their future plans and to map out a programme accordingly. He keeps himself on good terms with the boxer's parents, should he be under-age, and while he may not welcome the appearance of a girl friend, he makes sure not to offend her, even coercing her into being an asset instead of a liability. He must also make sure that his fighter possesses a copy of the Board of Control Rules and Regulations and understands them, so that there is no risk of him falling foul of authority through ignorance.

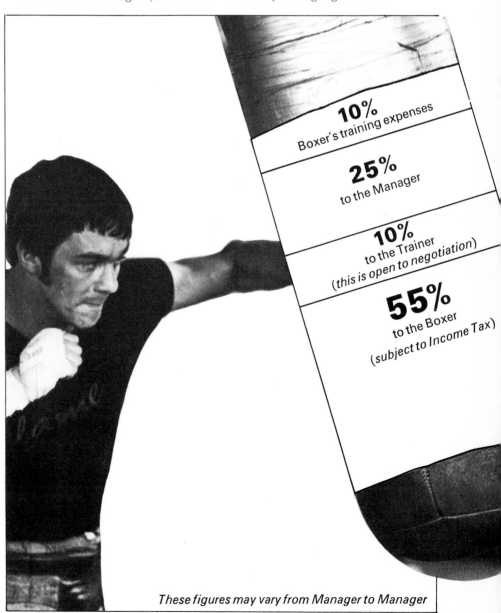

10%
Boxer's training expenses

25%
to the Manager

10%
to the Trainer
(*this is open to negotiation*)

55%
to the Boxer
(*subject to Income Tax*)

These figures may vary from Manager to Manager

THE MANAGER
The Big Day

The most important days in a manager's life are those when his boxer is taking part in a contest, either in a minor bout or a major event, both of which require his full and undivided attention. The day previous he has satisfied himself that his boxer is fully attuned for the ordeal ahead, both mentally and physically and that, if a stipulated weight is required, the boxer has reached that poundage in good time. Some managers have the boxer staying at his own home overnight or at the home of his trainer, not only to keep an eye on him, but also to provide an atmosphere most in keeping with the occasion. If travelling to another town for a contest or going abroad, the manager must ensure that they stay in the same hotel, having checked beforehand that everything the boxer will need in the ring is in good order and nothing left behind. It is essential that the boxer's kit contains two pairs of shorts of different colours so that he does not step into the ring wearing the same colour as his opponent, this being a standing order to avoid confusion both for the referee and the spectators.

If the match of the moment is taking place in their own vicinity, the manager or the trainer, or both, will collect the fighter from his home in good time so that he reaches the weighing-in venue at 1 o'clock, the usual time for such ceremonies and to which the public is normally invited to attend. First the boxer is examined by the Board of Control doctor, who gives him a general overhaul to ensure that he is fit to take part in a contest. The doctor knows just what to test and look for in an exercise that demands the utmost in stamina and endurance and he makes sure that there is nothing untoward that would affect the boxer harmfully whilst in the ring.

The boxers are then weighed by an official of the Board of Control, sometimes having to strip naked to make the required weight. The Inspector has the power to inspect the contracts for

Very often a manager of boxers finds it more convenient to use the gymnasium office for business purposes, any matches being made through the medium of the telephone. At the gymnasium he is in the centre of the current situation in the Fight Game, meeting promoters, and the managers, trainers, etc. and the fighting men themselves. It is also a most suitable place where he can meet and converse with his own boxers, whether they are in or out of training.

THE MANAGER

the contest and satisfy himself that the stipulated weight is not exceeded. He must also make certain that each boxer has an up-to-date licence. Should the boxer be over-weight he is given up to an hour in which to take off any surplus. He does this by putting on extra clothing and skipping, or in the case of an ounce or so, by massage, no resource being made to visit a sauna or turkish bath. If the over-weight boxer cannot reduce sufficiently to satisfy the inspector and his opponent's manager, then either he pays a forfeit to the other boxer or the fight is cancelled. There was an occasion when a fighter removed his false teeth in order to make the required weight and another who merely visited the toilet. If the boxer has had to starve himself the day previous or go without liquid intake for some hours in order to pass the scales, he can be given a flask of sustaining soup before going off to get a solid meal, as he will not be called upon to make weight again before entering the ring some seven or eight hours later.

It is then up to the manager to see that his boxer rests – even sleeps – until it is time to leave for the arena, perhaps having nothing more than a cup of tea. In the early days of glove-fighting, especially in America, fighters were sometimes compelled to weigh-in at ringside, while it was a smart move on a manager's part if he could set the weight for a contest at a poundage that was easy for his boxer to make, but for which the opponent would have to make a considerable and weakening reduction. This happened in the famous lightweight championship match between Joe Gans, the titleholder, and Oscar (Battling) Nelson at Goldfield in Nevada in 1906, when the challenger was able to force the champion into making a drastic reduction that proved injurious to his health and was always considered the cause of his death from consumption at the early age of 36.

Whilst it is compulsory for each boxer, no matter what size, to be weighed prior to a contest, it will be appreciated that weight-making does not apply to the heavyweights unless

The manager, Denny Mancini, consults trainer-second-instructor as to the procedure for the day.

Jimmy Revie, former British featherweight champion, gives some advice to one of his boxers.

Weighing a boxer who has to make a certain poundage at the Thomas a'Beckett gymnasium in London's Old Kent Road.

THE MANAGER

1

2

3

4

5

6

7

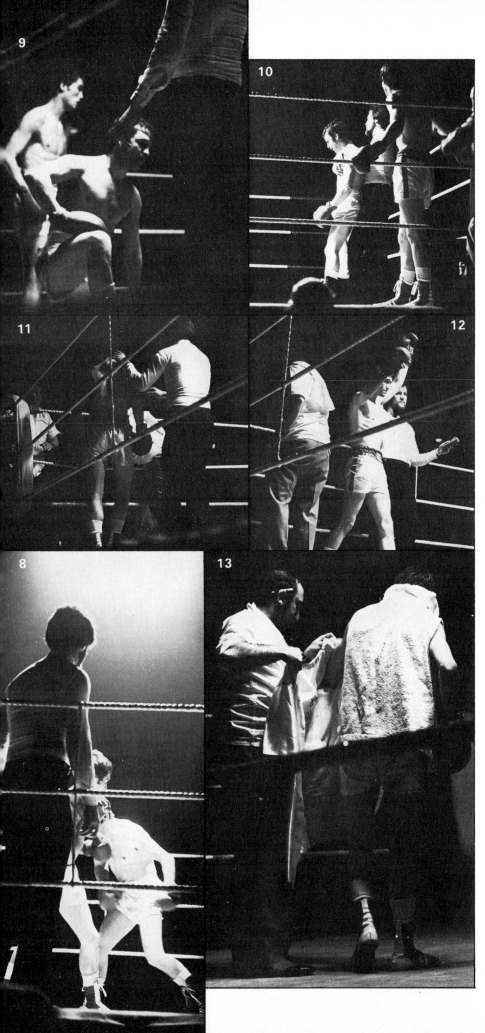

by special arrangement between the two sides, nor is it of great importance if there is a pound or two difference between men of those categories from welterweight upwards. From flyweight to lightweight, however, differences in weight should be confined to ounces and it is up to a manager not to take a contest in which his boxer will be called upon to concede a considerable amount of weight, and also, when he realises that his fighter is growing out of one class into another, that he allows him to move into the next division even if he has reached a title-challenging place in the lighter class. To keep a boxer down in weight merely to contest a championship is both wrong and unintelligent.

The manager accompanies his boxer to the arena and sees him safely installed in his dressing-room. He again checks his gear, takes personal possession of his gum-shield, sees that his hands are bandaged efficiently and in accordance with the regulations, keeps out anyone who is likely to disturb the boxer's peace of mind and generally safeguards him against any adverse contingency until the time comes to accompany him into the ring.

In the corner he presides over the lacing on of the gloves and quietly gives the fighter any last minute advice he deems necessary, if only to keep him mentally attuned to the task at hand. During the interval between the rounds he attends to or supervises the refreshing of his boxer and preparation for going out in good fettle for the next session. He must watch carefully to see that his boxer is fully fit to continue the contest and, if he feels there is no sense in carrying on, must summon the referee to the corner and ask permission to retire his fighter from the contest.

1. The boxer's hands are taped and bandaged in the dressing room.
2. The manager inspects the gloves to be used in the contest.
3. Climbing up the steps into the ring.
4. The start of the contest.
5. Referee keenly watching the infighting
6. During each interval the number board is shown to donate progress of the contest.
7. The referee keeps a close eye on a brisk attack.
8. The Third Man keeps on the move to watch the exchanges.
9. Referee orders boxer to neutral corner before taking up count from timekeeper.
10. Hurt boxer is escorted to his corner.
11. Referee goes to opposite corner and
12. Raises arm of winning boxer.
13. Boxer puts on dressing-robe prior to leaving the ring at the finish.

THE MANAGER

Of course, he is aided during the intervals by others, including a second supplied by the promoter. Usually the manager assumes the role of chief second, but should he appoint someone else in this capacity, he must not over-rule any decision that is made. If he is not the chief second, he can still give assistance in the corner if he so desires.

After the contest it is his duty to collect the purse money from the promoter, sometimes it being more convenient to wait until the next day, unless they are travelling home overnight. After a contest it is better for the boxer to remain in an hotel for the night and get a complete rest, rather than undertake a long and tiring journey when his energy and stamina have been exhausted in the ring. The manager must then prepare a statement of accounts and present it to the boxer together with the money due to him.

If a manager makes a full-time job of managing boxers, it is obvious that he needs more than one to occupy his time and provide a livelihood, unless he has under contract a champion capable of commanding large purses for each appearance. It is also necessary to be on the look-out for new blood as a boxer's career is limited in length of time and things can happen to cause his retirement from the Fight Game. The manager must therefore attend as many amateur tournaments as he can because these are the nurseries from which the professionals are recruited. He may also employ agents to be on the watch for likely material; youngsters who show promise of developing into worthwhile performers in the paid ranks.

If he has gained a reputation as a good and go-ahead manager, boxers will come to him by recommendation, or a member of his stable may introduce a younger brother. Some managers advertise in periodicals devoted to Boxing, inviting unattached boxers and amateurs who are considering the prospect of turning professional to contact them. He may even buy a boxer's contract from another manager, but only with the full agreement of the boxer and the approval of the Board of Control. It is sometimes in a boxer's interest for such a transfer to take place, especially if it is thought that more progress will result because the buying manager has greater opportunities and better contacts, but all must be done in a mutually agreeable manner.

Famous Managers

Jack Kearns. Known as 'Doc' Kearns because he always carried a small black bag into the corner containing his needs for administering to a fighter. Brought Jack Dempsey from a small-time fighter out in the sticks to the heavyweight championship of the world. Together they earned millions of dollars and in 1921 were associated in the first so-called Million Dollar Gate in the match between Dempsey and Carpentier at Boyles' 30 Acres, New Jersey. Kearns also managed Mickey Walker, who won both the welter and middleweight world titles, the pair garnering a fortune between them, and Joey Maxim, who he brought to England to take the light-heavyweight title from Freddie Mills.

Francois Descamps. Most famous of all French managers who found Georges Carpentier as a small boy and 'adopted' him. Taught him *La Boxe Anglaise*, then becoming all the rage in France, and took him from the age of 13 through every weight division until he fought for the heavyweight championship of the world against Jack Dempsey, by which time Carpentier, who had been out of the ring through war service for four years, was 27. It was a father-son partnership and several times in Georges' youth, Descamps never hesitated to stop a fight when he saw his boxer was being severely punished. Won an important fight by entering the ring and claiming that his boxer had been fouled.

Ted Broadribb. Boxed as 'Young Snowball' because of his very fair hair, but was far more successful as a manager, boasting that he had taken his boys to the championship in each of the original eight weight divisions. Brought Freddie Mills from obscurity to win the world light-heavyweight title and took Tommy Farr to a fight with Joe Louis for the heavyweight crown. Managed Nel Tarleton, Harry and Dick Corbett, Jack Hood and Johnny Williams, all of whom became British champions.

Joe Jacobs. American-Jewish manager noted for saying: "We should have stood in bed" after one of his fighters had lost a close decision. Won the world's heavyweight championship for Max Schmeling by entering the ring and bullying the referee and both judges into agreeing that his man had been fouled, the only occasion when the title has been won by a man on the canvas. Went to Nazi Germany to collect his cut when Schmeling fought there and on returning was upbraided by his countrymen for being photographed while giving the Nazi salute in the ring. Excused his behaviour by saying that it did not count as he had the fingers of his other hand crossed behind his back.

William A. Brady. The only man to manage two world heavyweight champions. A theatrical impressario by

profession, he chanced upon former bank clerk, Jim Corbett who had just won the world heavyweight title from John L. Sullivan, and put him into a play called 'Gentleman Jack', in which the boxer proved more than a passable actor. Taking over Corbett's affairs, he skilfully kept him on the stage and away from his most persistent challenger, Bob Fitzsimmons, for five years, a most lucrative period for both. When Corbett lost his title, Brady managed his novice sparring-partner, Jim Jeffries, and successfully took him through to a fight with Fitzsimmons which Jeffries won in eleven rounds. He even promoted a contest in New York to bring his fighter more into prominence.

Dan Sullivan. As manager and matchmaker at the famous 'Ring' at Blackfriars in South London, he was in a unique position to obtain and manage boxers. His two most famous were Len Harvey, whom he took over at the age of 17 and brought along to become known as 'Britain's Wonder Boxer' and on to the British middleweight title, and Jack Doyle, the flamboyant Irish heavyweight, who became an amazing box-office draw.

Jimmy Johnston. Famous American manager who made a speciality of looking after the interests of visiting British boxers. Noted for his eloquence and wordy battles with other managers during a contest, in particular, 'Dumb' Dan Morgan, equally verbatious. Johnston managed Ted (Kid) Lewis and Morgan looked after Jack Britton,

a noted New Yorker, and this pair fought a record twenty times, each of which provided a slanging match for their mentors. Johnston tried hard in his efforts to make Phil Scott, the British champion, into becoming world heavyweight titleholder, but just failed. Later he was appointed matchmaker to Madison Square Garden, the famous New York boxing arena.

Gus D'Amato. Brought Floyd Patterson from the 1952 Olympic Games to the heavyweight championship of the world, then carefully chose his opponents through four lucrative title fights, keeping him out of the reach of the International Boxing Club in New York whom he did not trust. When Patterson lost his title to Ingemar Johansson, D'Amato encouraged him to try and regain it which he did, so becoming the first-ever boxer to twice win the heavyweight crown. Much criticised, but in my book, a courageous and conscientious manager.

TRAINING

The gymnasium is an essential part of a boxer's training, both for the purpose of attaining physical perfection as required by a fighting man, but also for the development of footwork and ringcraft, fistic technique and skill. All places where the sport has a popular following or where a fistic star resides, have a gymnasium, some maintained by a former boxer, others by athletic clubs, occasionally in communal social centres. In Britain, however, they are found on public-house premises where the landlord is an ardent boxing supporter – either in a basement or a room over the bar, perhaps in an adjacent building belonging to the premises. Here a trainer/caretaker is installed, whose duty it is to keep the place clean and tidy, collect dues from the boxers for its use and maintain the equipment in first-class order. Publicans are noted for being strong supporters of Boxing and naturally they benefit, especially when champions or near champions are using the facilities he provides. The licensed victuallers trade has had close alliance with the Fight Game right from the days of the Prize Ring and some British pubs have been named after famous knuckle fighters of the past.

Training and boxing instruction in America is superior to anywhere else in the world because boxers in U.S.A. make it a full-time profession. This dedication influences South American boxers, Mexico and the Far East, all of which produce the most durable fighters and the hardest hitters. In Europe, the German, Italian and Spanish boxers undergo a more severe training routine than in G.B., France and Belgium, Denmark and Holland.

Even when boxers have no definite contest in view, they will pay one or two visits a week to their usual gymnasium in order to keep in fighting trim. Here they are watched over by their managers, trainers and seconds, while promoters and their matchmakers or agents keep an observant eye in the non-stop search for talent. In fact, the gymnasium becomes the general meeting place for the fight fraternity, where business transactions are made, the current situation discussed and where the important factor of keeping informed of what is going on can be maintained.

Each gymnasium must contain a ring which vary in size according to the space available. As near as possible these conform with the regulation size, 14 feet square, and the nearer the training ring is like the ring in which the forthcoming contest is to be fought, the better. The importance of this must be obvious and I can recall an instance where a famous French champion, who was to defend his title in London, sent over an agent to measure up the ring in which he was to fight and then had a replica built in which to train. It was a precaution that paid off because he won a sensational victory in 74 seconds of the opening round.*

When the boxer reaches his training-quarters, either around mid-day or in the evening, whichever suits him best, although the morning period is the more popular, he changes into his working kit, shorts and a sweat shirt if he is already near the contracted weight, or in heavy leotards, shirt and sweater, if he has to reduce. He is now ready to go through a full work-out and although there is no set routine for this, he usually warms-up with several rounds of shadow-boxing, time being kept by his mentor, so that he spends three minutes of this essential part of his preparation, then takes a minute's rest, just as if he were engaged in a real contest. If he is in the novice class and boxing over two-minute rounds, then the time is adjusted accordingly.

The term 'shadow-boxing' is somewhat misleading, although it may seem that the boxer is sparring with a shadow. Actually he indulges in fantasy fighting, imagining he has an opponent in the ring with him and trying out all the moves and punches in his repertoire, varying what he does as much as possible, his mind concentrating on getting the better of his phantom rival, even ducking, side-stepping or slipping imaginary blows aimed at him. Just before the end of each round, his trainer will call out 'last ten', which means that ten seconds remain, whereupon the boxer puts on a spurt and goes all out in a final assault on his unseen adversary.

The shadow-boxing is followed by actual sparring, again in rounds of three minutes duration with a minute's rest in between, big gloves being worn to deaden the punches exchanged and so avoiding physical damage. Sometimes the boxer will wear gloves the same weight as those he will use in the ring while his spar-mate puts on a head-guard to minimise the power of the punches he has to take. Sparring partners vary. Usually they are of the same weight as the boxer in training, sometimes heavier, to enable him to go all out in his punching, sometimes lighter to increase hitting speed and pace of footwork. Two or three rounds are devoted to sparring, more if the trainer thinks necessary, but usually the time allotted to the whole session adds up to the number of scheduled rounds for the forthcoming contest or a few more, but rarely less. At intervals the trainer will call on the sparring-partner to make as near a real fight of it as possible, putting in spirited bursts of aggression to keep the boxer on the alert for a sudden attack.

It is also important that at least one of the sparring-partners has a style similar to that of the forthcoming

*Carpentier v. Beckett, Holborn Stadium, 4.12.1919.

Shadow-boxing is an invaluable part of a boxer's training because his 'opponent' exists only in his mind and he contrives to outwit him with moves and punches both at long and short range in fantasy.

TRAINING

opponent and, in addition, the wise manager will endeavour to obtain the services of a boxer who has recently fought the man who will be in the opposite corner on the night of the fight.

Such careful details have match-winning qualities and, after all, that is what it is all about. Some boxers make better spar-mates than others and those who can bring out the best in the man in training and get him into peak condition for the fight in hand, can earn good money when they are not preparing for a bout themselves. Equally, a boxer in training very often welcomes the opportunity to spar with another who is getting himself into shape, even if in another weight division.

Next comes a spell on the overhead platform punch-ball for working up speed and rhythm, the boxer beating out a tattoo that tunes-up co-ordination of hand and eye and provides keen reflex action. The swinging ball, suspended from the ceiling and fastened to the floor, is another toning-up appliance, while the heavy bag enables the boxer to develop his punching-power and he can work on this at long range for practising his leading punches, or at close-quarters to indulge in infighting. Ground exercises, or calisthenics, come next with the boxer going through a variety of movements. Press-ups on the hands in a prone position, cycling with the legs whilst supine. Bringing the legs over the head and rotating the body whilst tapping on the floor with the toes; hands behind neck and rotating the body whilst sitting, also bending forwards and touching the toes with outstretched arms. All these floor exercises are for the purpose of keeping the body supple and at the same time building up a strong muscular abdominal wall against body punches, whilst strengthening the legs, arms, neck and shoulder muscles.

In standing position, swinging the arms downwards to touch the left toe with the finger-tips of the right hand, and vice versa, in both cases without bending the knees, is another fine body-tuning exercise that boxers favour.

The Medicine Ball, a heavy inflated leather ball, is also used in a variety of ways for alertness and shoulder power when thrown from trainer to boxer, sometimes being bounced on a boxer's abdomen for further strengthening and resistance against body blows. A train-

ing session usually ends up with a skipping spell, timed in rounds, each one finishing with a very rapid twirling of the rope. Skipping is essential for gaining lightness of movement, regular breathing and the vital co-ordination of hands and feet.

No trainer worthy of the name will subject his boxer to what is known as a 'drying-out' process (going without food and drink, also excessive sweating) in order to make a specified weight. If the boxer is having difficulty in this respect, it is far better for him to give up the projected contest rather than be submitted to this injurious ordeal.

On occasions, such as when training for a championship contest, a boxer will go away to a country or seaside place to train, staying at an inn that has its own gymnasium, or using a local amateur club's premises. Some men, according to their make-up and temperament, like a complete change of scene and society in quiet surroundings; it ensures greater concentration for the task ahead. This was practised far more in the past in England, before the smokeless zone era, and many

places became famous as favourite training camps for leading boxers. That they do not exist today can be due to the change in public house operating, the lack of space in modern pubs for the provision of the large area required for a gymnasium, or because of the dwindling number of boxers, from something like 4,000 in the 1920's and 30's, to a bare 300 at the present time. In America, where the standard of professional boxing is higher than in the rest of the world, there remain established training camps, some of them in the clean air of the hills, or in lakeside surroundings, far away from the pollution of the cities.

Apart from the apparatus already mentioned, the fully-equipped gymnasium can have a set of weights and bars for general body-building, although weight-lifting, as such, is shunned by boxers as being conducive to muscle-binding. Climbing wall bars are also useful for arm and leg development, while a rowing machine has a similar purpose. A set of scales are a must in any gymnasium, the boxer checking his weight both before and

Using the ring, developing footwork, fighting on and off the ropes, in and out of corners and practising punches and combinations. Alan Minter, British middleweight champion and winner outright of a Lonsdale Belt, goes through the ritual of Shadow boxing.

after his work-out. Shower-bath facilities are also essential for the man in training.

The person in charge of the premises is usually supplied with a small office. Here he has a variety of items that might be wanted, such as spare bandages, adhesive tape, a first-aid kit; with ball and bag punching gloves and clean towels he can lend out. He also books boxers in for a series of training periods on specific days and at regular times, so there is no waiting, and he keeps the place as busy as he can for as much of the day as possible. Most managers do their business from their own homes, but the gymnasium provides a useful sub-office and he can always use the telephone for incoming and outgoing calls.

55

TRAINING
The Trainer's Role

Of course, apart from the boxers, the most important person who uses the gymnasium, is the trainer, whether he is looking after his own fighter, working for a manager or, as custodian of the gym, he also holds a trainer's or second's licence and is therefore qualified to give help or advice to any young unattached boy, or one who happens to find himself on his own. There are three types of trainers: those who are primarily physical conditioners who supervise the exercises and use of apparatus; those whose chief concern is to teach Boxing – the professors of the Noble Art, and the man who concentrates on being a Second, going into the corner with a boxer and administering to him before, during and after a contest.

Sometimes all three qualities are combined in one individual and usually the physical trainer also assumes the role of second, while the Instructor confines himself to his trade. While trainers are licenced by the Boxing Authority for an annual fee and seconds also, there is no separate recognition of Instructors in a singular manner, it being considered that their duties are covered by those of the trainer and second, yet the teaching of Boxing is a specialised profession and without an Instructor young boxers would be left to pick up the rudiments as they go along, a far more precarious way of learning.

The Instructor goes into the training ring with the boxer and spars with him, but not in the manner of another boxer who is acting as a sparring-partner. He tells the novice to aim a left jab, blocks it, either with an open hand, an unclenched glove or a specially devised pad which he slips on and uses as a target for the pupil. He makes him try using the left hand in a full repertoire

The trainer bears the full responsibility for bringing his boxer to the peak of fighting fitness. He is the man on whom the boxer relies, not only in the gymnasium, but also as a second during the contest itself.

56

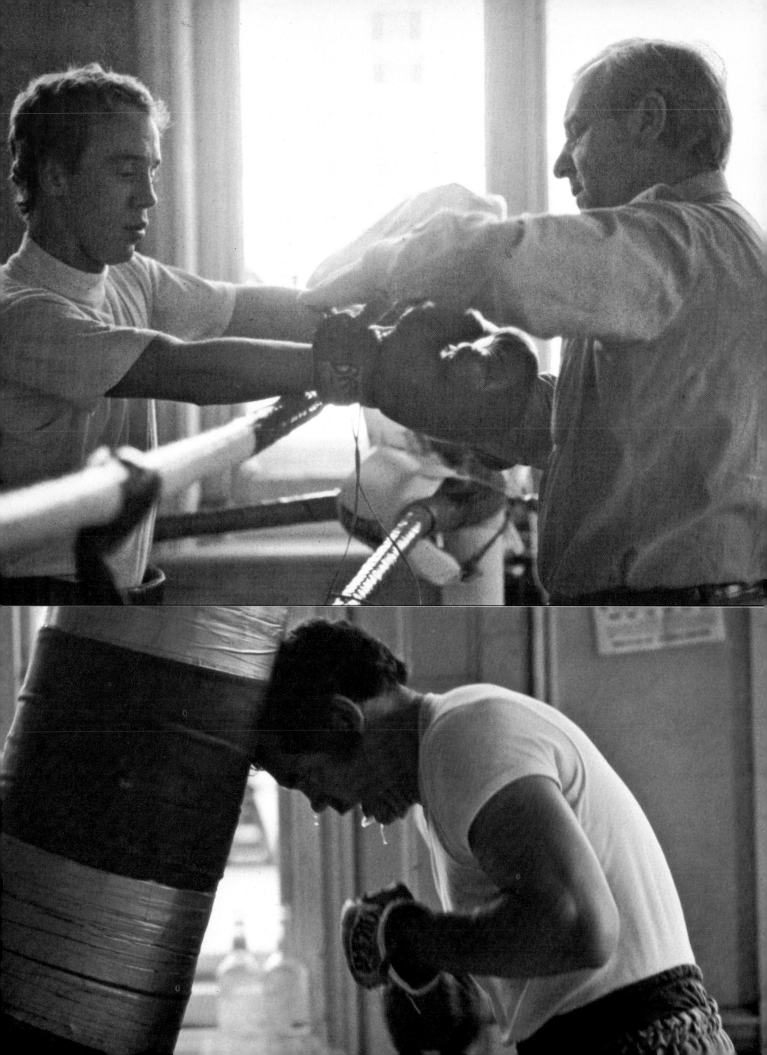

TRAINING

of moves, calling out the punches or merely moving the 'target glove'. He then does the same for the right hand, then both hands together to teach the boxer how to develop combination punching, following one blow with another in short bursts from a variety of angles.

Switching to defence, the Instructor tests his pupil's reflexes and alertness by nominating a punch for which he expects the boxer to provide a barrier, and then leading with something entirely different – a deceiving move from which the pupil learns not to be taken by surprise. By this means the boxer becomes skilful in feinting, i.e. intimating a move, then delivering an unexpected punch from another direction altogether.

Former boxers delight in talking about their past fights, particularly those they won and, telling me of a famous victory, one said : "I just *nodded* him a left and knocked him out with a straight right to the chin." The 'nod' was the feint and his opponent had

tried to beat him to the punch with a left lead of his own. In doing so he had left himself open to a right cross and that was that. "Be first" is an instruction that is hammered into young boxers from the start because of its psychological advantage and effect. Famous Joe Gans won the world lightweight title by knocking out Frank Erne in a single round. "I kept aiming rights at him, but he moved his head just enough to make me miss. So I tossed a right at the spot where I thought he would move into it – and so he did," was the Old Master's simple explanation of his sensational victory.

Instructors must also teach novices how to react when hurt – covering up, boxing on the retreat, using the ropes when trapped against them, and how to get out of a tight corner. A lot of young boxers learn from sparring with others, but they have to be correctly taught the basic moves and sharpened up both in attack and defence. Of great importance is the ability to slip into a

clinch, either when hurt, to offset a persistent and energetic attack, or for the purpose of infighting. Holding is an offence that can earn disqualification, but is a very effective way of tying-up an opponent and so preventing him from bombarding the body at close-quarters.

A well-known trick of the trade is to hold on the 'blind' side of the referee, indeed to render an opponent harmless by holding with one hand and getting in the sly punch with the other. It is when the other man retaliates in like measure that the referee observes what is going on, breaks the boxers and administers a caution to the one he thinks is the chief offender. 'Pickles' Douglas, one of the foremost referees of his day, told me he could always tell which man was doing the holding when

Managers, trainers and/or seconds give instructions from outside the ring during sparring sessions, exalting the spar-mate to vary the work-out as much as possible, encouraging the boxer in training to try out and master certain moves and punches.

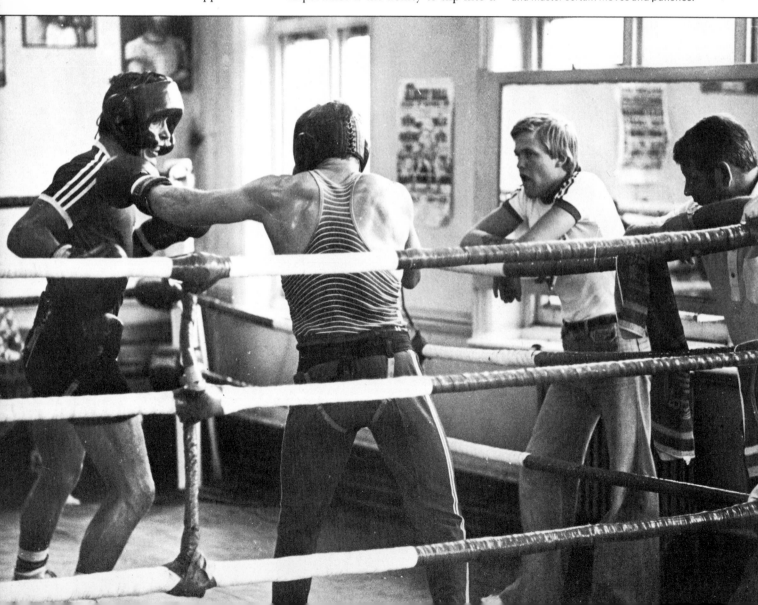

the pair were in a clinch, not only if one was struggling to free himself, but by the fact that the holder was on the flat of his heels, whereas the man being held was pulled on to his toes.

Brief holding is often condoned by a referee when it is purely a defensive measure, but he will caution the boxer if he thinks fit. Prolonged holding leads to wrestling, with the captive man trying to get free, and if an offending boxer flagrantly continues to break this rule, he renders himself liable to being ruled out of the contest. Len Harvey, who held the world grip record, would restrain the efforts of an aggressive fighter intent on body punching by grasping him firmly before pushing him off into long range exchanges at which he excelled. Jock McAvoy, who met Harvey four times over fifteen rounds told me that his biceps on both arms were black and blue for days after each contest with the famous Cornishman. Muhammad Ali (Cassius Clay) also made an art of holding, especially in the latter part of his career. When he was defending his world heavyweight title against Karl Mildenberger in Frankfurt, referee Teddy Waltham sharply informed him that he was holding. "With which hand?" cheekily enquired the champion, and looked startled when the reply came: "Both – and don't do it."

Another important lesson in infighting is to get what is known as the 'inside position', that is to get your own arms within those of your opponent's, thus giving yourself a body target on which to indulge in free hitting, while the other man has to go round your elbows in order to score and can be guilty of punching illegally, either to the back or in the region of the kidneys. It also lessens the power he can put into his blows. A smart and knowledgeable Instructor knows all these dodges and passes them on to his pupil, especially such moves as turning an opponent into your own punches by grasping his elbow and moving it one way or the other with the open glove and then hooking or swinging to the body or head. The avoidance of punches is as important as delivering them and the Instructor's task is to teach his pupil every possible move that can be made, to duck, dodge, draw away from, side-step and block all the blows that come his way, yet at the same time know just what to do when caught by a delivery that comes out of the blue.

Perhaps the most important thing an Instructor should teach his pupil is to punch with the back knuckles of the fist. Far too many young boxers are inclined to hit with the open glove, brought about principally by trying to extend the reach. It is a bad habit that if not corrected can prove disastrous. These slaps may sound like heavy punches to the far-off fans, but they do not earn points from an efficient referee and can lead to disqualification, as failure to close the gloves when striking is deemed a foul delivery. Incorrect hitting of any sort can cause damage to the hands and without efficient tools the boxer has no hope of success. Striking with the side of the fist can

TRAINING

Work on the heavy-bag provides punching power and enables a boxer to develop and work out combination-punching sequences.

Sparring-partners are engaged who closely resemble the forthcoming opponents in size, weight and style. The boxers make these sparring sessions to time and as real as possible, with the spar-mate assuming the minor role. Sometimes the trainer will order the men to 'mix-it' during the last ten seconds of the training round – 'last ten' being a notification that the round is nearing an end and calling for a last spurt.

break a thumb, while defective punching may cause finger fractures and misplacement of the metacarpal bones of the hand.

The Trainer's job, apart from supervising the apparatus work and free exercising, is to make sure that his boxer is as perfect inside as he is in outward appearance. Without the proper functioning of the inner-man, the boxer cannot reach physical perfection, so his diet must be watched carefully, especially if he is making a specific weight, and foods avoided that may clog the system, constipation being the biggest evil a man in training can encounter. Strangely enough, this happens to the most earnest athletes. It is also the trainer's duty to have a

thorough knowledge of physiology and to be able to inform the young boxer how the human anatomy works and the best way to keep it functioning correctly.

The Second has a highly-important job, but as his work is confined to the dressing-room at the arena and the corner during a contest, his duties will be dealt with in the chapter appertaining to the Ring. But he will always be found in the gymnasium, because he cannot carry out his work in the corner unless he is also a trainer, and to some extent, an instructor also. Therefore he must be well acquainted with the current Boxing scene and be capable of correcting and advising a fighter during a training session.

TRAINING

At this point it would be appropriate to explain why a man who administers to a boxer before a contest and during the intervals between each round should be called a 'second'. Seconding is a term accepted without query by the average fight fan and all those connected with the Fight Game. Whereas referees, timekeepers and announcers are known by names that describe their vocations, the origin of the Second is generally unknown. It comes from the Prize Ring, as do so many words and terms that have crept into the English language.

Prize Fights of importance sometimes took months, even a year or more before they could be finalised and the men brought together. The venue, generally in the open-air, was kept secret until the last possible moment to avoid interference from the police, then the word was spread, perhaps tickets sold in taverns and at fairs, and the day

before the long-awaited battle The Fancy and all the followers of bare-knuckle bruising would make their way to the chosen battle site by whatever means they could, some travelling many miles by horseback, coach or cart, and to the nearest station when the railways were built.

To avoid disturbance, if by chance the contest ended quickly or disappointingly, a secondary bout was arranged and advertised, the principals involved being men from the opposing sides who had perhaps acted as sparring-partners or helped to prepare one of the contestants in the main event. Apart from furnishing a bout if called upon to do so, their presence was also required to give all possible aid to the fighter whom they had assisted in training and they were allowed in the corner after each round, either to provide a knee on which the fighter could sit and rest, sponge him down,

To develop a boxer's reflexes, the trainer uses a special hand-pad which serves as a moving target; the instructor using it as if it were an opponent's head; shortening or extending the distance, at the same time encouraging the boxer to hit at it with jabs, hooks, crosses, upper-cuts or straight punches as he calls them.

and generally revive him for the next round. They might even have to help him to come up and toe the line if he was in an exhausted state, but they were not permitted to remain in the ring during the actual exchanges.

As they were to take part in a second contest, they became known as Seconds, and when in due time their work in an administrative capacity evolved into an entirely separate role, the name continued to be used by force of habit and these men, whose job it is to keep their boxer in the fight by repairing his wounds and reviving his stamina, have been known as 'seconds' ever since.

MANOR PLACE BATHS
SMITH v MOORE
SMITH v GRIFFITHS
GWILLIAM v ROOMS
CAMMISS v WALLACE
O'MARA v GWILLIAM
AMPRO
ONDON
NO SMOKIN

TRAINING

Using weights to strengthen the biceps.

The strengthening of the mid-section muscles is of paramount importance to a boxer.

Weight training forms part of the boxer's general fitness build-up and is done under supervision.
The exercise shown here is the parallel squat, a support under the heels is used to provide balance.

This exercise known as the 'Fencers Lunge' is to mobilize the hip joints. The thigh is pressed towards the ground with the trunk kept upright.

Hip exercise to help increase mobility.

TRAINING

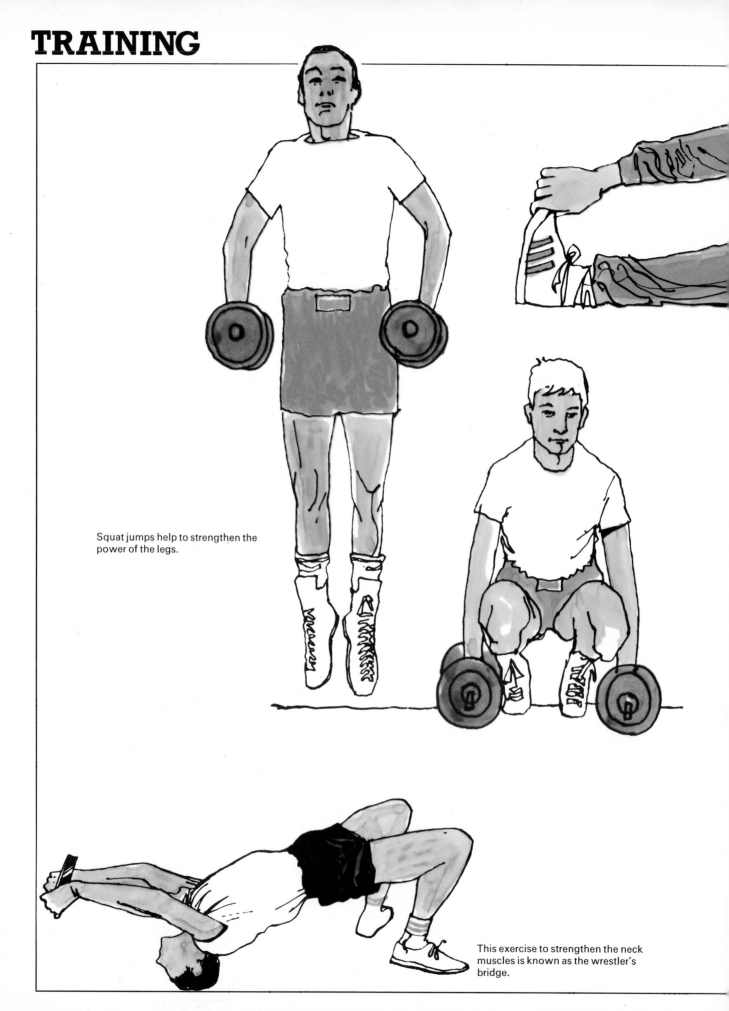

Squat jumps help to strengthen the power of the legs.

This exercise to strengthen the neck muscles is known as the wrestler's bridge.

Any exercise to keep the lower back supple and enabling the boxer to exercise the joint of the ankle at the same time are of great value. This exercise should be carried out after a work-out when the muscles are warmed up.

Skipping forms a major part of any boxer's training programme.

Alternately pressing arms back to increase suppleness of the shoulder muscles.

Rotating the trunk in a circular movement with the arms extended above the head helps keep the spine supple.

THE CONTEST

On the day of the contest the boxer and his entourage, manager, trainer, chief second, arrive at the arena at the time stipulated in his contract and makes his way immediately to the dressing-rooms. Here he is met by the Whip, a man specially appointed by the promoter to (a) see that every boxer on the programme has duly arrived, (b) to steer each one to the particular dressing-room allocated to him, (c) to inform the boxer in what order he is due to appear in the ring, first, second – perhaps last, although the fighter taking part in the principal bout of the evening usually expects to be ready by about 9 p.m., and (d) to make sure he has all the necessary requirements, including the two pairs of shorts of different colours, the ones that differ from his opponent's being the chosen pair.

Opponents are not put in the same dressing-room in the major promotions, although this may happen in the smaller arenas where only one changing place is available, then they are kept apart as much as possible. The main event fighters may have rooms to themselves, but usually several boxers share, their names being posted on a slip of paper attached to the door, so that pressmen can locate them before a contest and friends find them afterwards. The Whip must also make sure that every boxer is medically examined by the official Doctor and get a signature against the name of each man as having been passed fit to fight. In addition, it is essential that the doctor should make sure that the boxer is not suffering from any condition which may be aggravated by boxing, or that he has an infectious skin disease. The Whip must also give free access to the Board of Control's Inspector, whose duty it is to see for himself that the boxer appears to be in perfectly fit condition, and also to superintend the putting on of the hand bandages and adhesive tape. When he is satisfied that all is in order, he rubber-stamps the bandages which prevents them from being changed after his inspection. The bandages are for the protection of the hands and must not exceed 18 feet of 2-inch soft bandage for all weights, and/or 9 feet of 1-inch zinc oxide plaster tape for weights up to and including middleweight, and 11 feet for the light-heavy and heavyweight, in all cases these lengths are for each hand. The plaster tape must *not*, however, be applied over the knuckles.

If the boxer is going into the ring wearing his gloves, then the Inspector makes certain that these are in good condition and are not interfered with in any way until they are finally laced up and tied, a special elasticised covering attached to the glove being drawn over the knot. It is also the duty of the Inspector to see that each boxer has an up-to-date licence and that he is dressed properly for entry into the ring.

It is reasonable to understand why it is necessary for the bandaging of the hands and the putting on of the gloves to be carefully scrutinised by an impartial observer in an official capacity. In the so-called 'good old days' all manners of tricks were employed to gain an unfair advantage over an opponent, one of the worst being to dust the bandages beforehand with powdered Plaster of Paris. Then, just before putting on the glove the hand would be dipped into a bucket of water with the result that after a few rounds the fist would become brick hard so that blows were far more damaging, cutting an opponent's face to ribbons. The giant cowboy, Jess Willard, accused Jack Dempsey of using reinforced bandages when he was knocked down seven times in the first round at Toledo in Ohio in 1919 and lost his championship after three rounds. Dempsey strongly denied this and provided proof that the allegation was untrue, but Willard continued to believe he had been unfairly treated up to the time of his death at the age of 87, 49 years later.

The watchfulness over the putting on of the gloves in the ring comes from another playful procedure of the past, when a beaten boxer and his followers would declare that the other man had slipped a horseshoe into his glove just prior to going into the ring. It might have happened, but I know of no specific instance. However, when Tiger Flowers was knocked out by Jack Delaney in two rounds in New York in 1925, the black boxer and his manager declared that the winner had inserted a piece of 'Irish Confetti' into his glove during the interval before the fatal round, meaning a small brass dumbbell which the wearer could grasp and so give himself lethal punching power. They made this allegation because they thought Flowers was too tough to be knocked out by anyone, even though he was only a middleweight, whereas Delaney was a stone heavier. They protested to the Boxing Commission so vehemently that a re-match was ordered which took place a few weeks later. This time Walk Miller, Flowers' manager, stood in Delaney's corner and watched his gloves being put on, then had someone to keep a sharp lookout between the rounds to see that nothing was slipped into them. Nothing was, but Delaney knocked the Tiger out again, this time in round four.

Having received a preliminary order of running, and satisfied himself that all is in order, the Whip waits until he receives a signal from the Promoter or Ring Master that it is time for the first pair to go into the ring, then he precedes them into the arena and marches them round to their respective corners. He then returns to the dressing-room to make sure that the next pair are gloved up and ready for action in

The call of "seconds out" leaves the referee in sole charge of the contest.

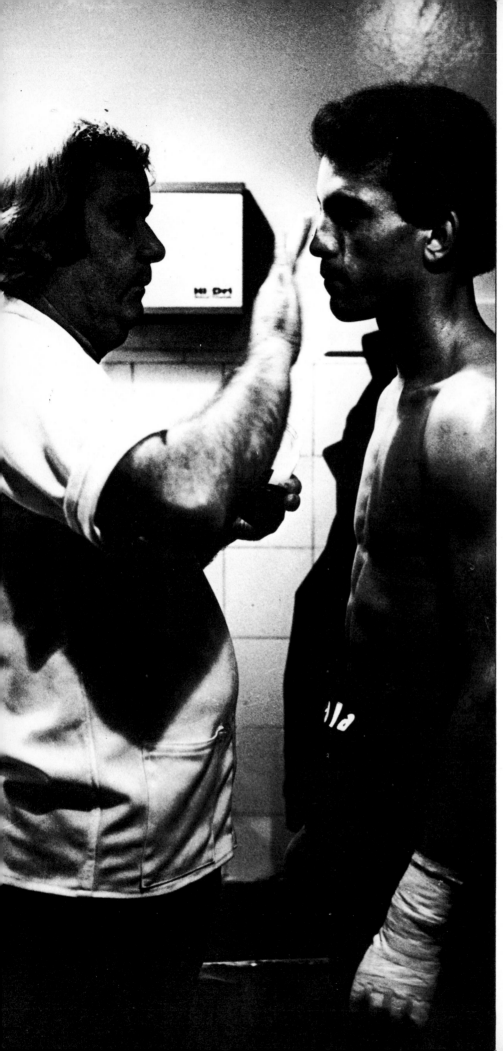

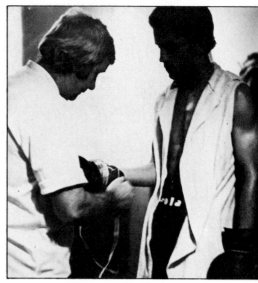

In the dressing room the tension mounts, the seconds caters to the needs of the boxer, taping the hands, applying vaseline, generally creating an air of calmness.

case the first contest is cut short by a knockout, a stoppage, or a disqualification.

As everyone knows, there are Whips in parliamentary procedure, and I hold the view that the term comes direct from the Prize Ring. In those turbulent days, when partisanship ran high and often uncontrolled, it was necessary for the organisers of a bare-knuckle battle to do all they could to prevent any ringside disturbance or rioting among the onlookers, not only for the protection of the wealthy patrons of the sport, but also to avoid complications with the police, seeing that they were involved in an illegal activity. To this end an inner and an outer ring were provided, the fighters occupying the inner roped square, while the outer was patrolled by a band of strong-arm men, usually boxers or ex-boxers, each armed with a horse-whip, their purpose being to restrain excited spectators from breaking through and interfering with the pugilists, by using their whips efficiently and effectively.

They became known as the Whips and quite understandably were treated with the utmost respect. If a secondary contest took place after the principal fight, for which no purse had been offered, these hired defenders of law and order would go round amongst the crowd, hat in one hand and whip in the other, to make a collection, especially if the 'seconds' had put up a good hard-hitting bout. This became known as a

The Ring

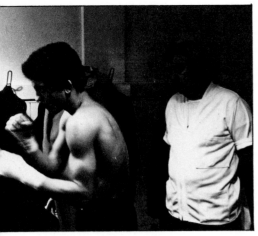

'Whip Round', a term commonly used nowadays when collecting up money to meet a cause or obligation. In modern Boxing the duty of the Whip is to keep a smooth-running continuity of fighters from the dressing-room to the ring itself.

The custom of making a collection for the boxers after a particularly pleasing contest remains to this day when spectators, especially in the small arenas and the membership clubs, throw notes and coins generously into the ring at the conclusion of an exciting bout. This money is shared equally by the boxers concerned and is known in the Fight Game as being a 'nobbins'. How it got this name is something of a mystery and I have never met anyone who has clearly defined its origins. It occurs to me that it may emanate from the fact that the early dispensers of such largesse were the noblemen who attended the Prize Fights, in other words 'the nobs', or it might date back earlier still to the days of the 'noble' a gold coin to the value of 6s. 8d. in the reign of Edward III, which strangely enough was the one-time set fee of a solicitor for writing a letter.

Another possible source comes from 'Lord' John Sanger, the renowned circus proprietor, in his colourful autobiography: *Seventy Years a Showman*, in which he tells how they would let an audience in free of charge for the first half of the programme, then the ring-master would announce: "In order to test your appreciation of our efforts, before we go on with the rest of the performance, the young men will go round with the hat." This is known in the profession as 'nobbing', and not a soul among the spectators, some two or three hundred, escaped being 'nobbed', whether they parted or not. Then the second half of the performance was proceeded with."

It may seem strange that the perfect square in which a boxing match takes place should be called a 'ring', but again the name emanates from Prize Ring times. In the very early days of bare-knuckle fighting, its exponents were usually two men who teamed up and went around the country visiting the village fairs, carrying with them a length of rope sufficient to make a large circle. They would select a pitch, invite the onlookers to form a circle, holding the rope as taut as possible, thus providing a ring in which they would demonstrate the Art of Self Defence, give an exhibition bout, and, if one was forthcoming, invite any fistically inclined, to come in and swap punches, either for fun or for a bet. Thus the place in which fighting men fought became known as The Ring and it was found necessary to stake out a square and use fastened ropes when the crowds grew in number for important matches and had to be kept under control, it having been found that in exciting moments the spectators holding the rope were apt to drop it or converge on the fighters thus causing uproar and chaos.

The size of the ring can vary, the rules stipulating that all contests are to be decided in a three-roped ring (sic), with the ropes joined in the centre at each side; not less than 14 feet or more than 20 feet square, and not less than 18 inches margin of floor outside the ropes. The floor of the ring must be covered with canvas over a safety-mat to be provided by the promoter and approved by the Board of Control. The corner posts that stand away from the ring ropes far enough to avoid a boxer being driven against one with the back of his head, must be effectively padded. It is the duty of the Inspector to see that the ropes have been strung sufficiently taut and it is not uncommon to find a boxer, especially a heavyweight testing these for himself before a contest by laying back on them.

As soon as he has climbed up the steps into his corner, the fighter sits down whilst awaiting the preliminaries to be gone through. These are quite elaborate and of long-standing, a ritual that adds to the glamorous and tense atmosphere that pervades in a boxing arena. Sometimes a boxer likes to sit in what has become the winning corner that evening and their managers will toss a coin for choice. Again, if the fight is taking place in the open-air, when the selection of the right corner can be of the utmost importance, especially if it is sunny, the same method of deciding is applied.

The gloves

The weight of the gloves used vary according to the size of the boxers: Six ounces each for flyweights to welters and eight ounces each for middleweights up to heavies. 'Breaking' the gloves by twisting, removal of padding by fingering and thumbing from the potential part of the glove, is prohibited and it is up to the Inspector to watch carefully to see that this is not done. A set of new gloves are provided by the Board of Control for championship matches and the Announcer (Master of Ceremonies) is handed a box containing them by the Whip. This is placed in the centre of the ring and the managers come up to select a pair, sometimes tossing a coin for first choice. It is the duty of the Announcer to receive from the Whip an up-to-date programme, showing any amendments that may have had to been made, also the weight of each fighter (as announced at the official 'Weigh-In'). He must also make sure that he identifies the boxers in each bout as soon as they enter the ring. He must also have his programme marked to show the name of the referee for each contest, and also make sure he knows the exact number of rounds to be fought for each contest and the duration of each round.

No contest must exceed 15 rounds or be of less than twelve minutes duration, except bouts between novices which can be restricted to eight minutes of actual boxing, i.e. four rounds of two-minutes each round. All championship contests must be fought over fifteen 'threes' and final-eliminating title bouts must go to twelve rounds of three minutes each. For contests of ten rounds and under, usually between up-and-coming boys and beginners in the professional ranks, the rounds are restricted to two minutes each.

THE CONTEST

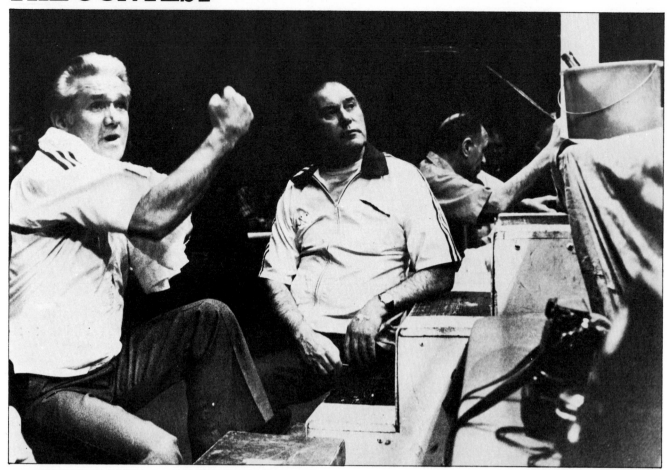

In the Corner

The most important man in a boxer's corner from all points of view, is the one nominated as the Chief Second. He can be the Manager, the Trainer or someone in whom the boxer has great faith and perhaps a special liking. Whoever he is, he has complete say, although there is usually general agreement as to what decisions are made. The number of seconds in a corner are restricted to four for all contests of more than six rounds, made up by the Chief Second, a House Second, provided by the promoter, and two others, one of whom is a specialist in dealing with facial injuries, especially lacerations around the eyes. He is generally known as the 'Cuts Man', his job being to staunch any bleeding. The equipment he takes into the cirner is restricted to the following items:

No stimulant other than cold water sprinkled on the body or used as a mouth wash may be employed and seconds are forbidden to use: Iron chloride solution, Monsol, ammoniated liniments for massage preliminary to a contest, or alcohol in any form. The number of seconds for a six or less rounds contest is limited to two, one of whom will be the House Second, whose duty it is to see that a water bottle, filled with clean drinking water, is in the corner prior to the start of a bout, also that a bowl is provided for the boxer to use after having a mouthwash, and to take this away, wash it out and replace it in clean condition during the interval between contests. He must also remove this bowl immediately the Timekeeper calls 'Seconds Out', together with the water bottle, which is usually laminated with tape to prevent it from slipping out of the hands.

The seconds wait to leap into the ring at the end of the round, valuable time can be lost if the teamwork is lacking.

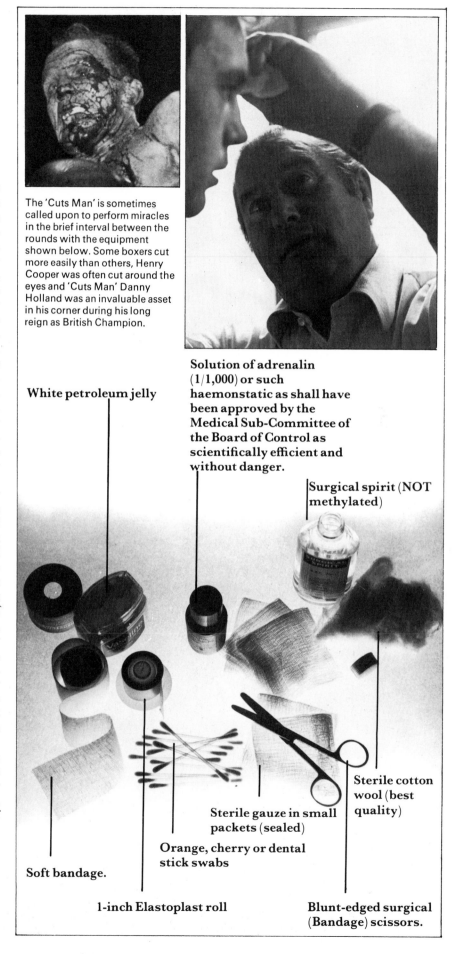

The 'Cuts Man' is sometimes called upon to perform miracles in the brief interval between the rounds with the equipment shown below. Some boxers cut more easily than others, Henry Cooper was often cut around the eyes and 'Cuts Man' Danny Holland was an invaluable asset in his corner during his long reign as British Champion.

White petroleum jelly

Solution of adrenalin (1/1,000) or such haemonstatic as shall have been approved by the Medical Sub-Committee of the Board of Control as scientifically efficient and without danger.

Surgical spirit (NOT methylated)

Sterile cotton wool (best quality)

Sterile gauze in small packets (sealed)

Orange, cherry or dental stick swabs

Soft bandage.

1-inch Elastoplast roll

Blunt-edged surgical (Bandage) scissors.

At the Ringside

At most professional Boxing shows, and particularly those of major importance, a narrow table runs all round the ringside for the use of the press, sometimes a second and even a third row is provided according to the nature of the main bout. Usually the first row is occupied by boxing writers who have been provided with telephones, and cameramen, these latter being intrepid characters who almost creep under the lower rope in order to get their shots. On one side, however, a space is reserved for the ringside officials; the Board of Control Steward who is in charge of the evening's proceedings, an Area representative, the official doctor, and the General Secretary of the Board of Control.

They sit either side of the Timekeeper with his bell or gong, and usually two stop watches – one to start and terminate the rounds and the other to record any knockdowns. The Referee is empowered to order a Timekeeper to 'Take Time Off' if he wishes to stop

1 Official Doctor
2 Board of Control Steward
3 Timekeeper
4 General Secretary of the Board of Control
5 Judge
6 Press
7 TV Commentator
8 Substitute Referee
9 Master of Ceremonies
  Red Corner
10 Second/Cuts Man
11 Chief Second/Manager
  Blue Corner
12 Chief Second/Trainer
13 Second/Cuts Man
14 Referee
15 Boxers
16 TV Cameraman
17 Press Photographer
18 Round Boy

The illustration shows the use of three judges, as on the continent, to deliver the decision. In the United States of America, Mexico and South America it is the referee with the assistance of two judges who arrive at the decision. In Britain and the majority of the Commonwealth countries the verdict is arrived at solely by the referee.
The size of the ring may vary between :
Minimum size : 14 square feet
Maximum size : 20 square feet

Generally the ring has three ropes around its perimeter, but four ropes may be used, for instance in the United States of America some States stipulate, and boxers themselves may request, the use of four ropes.

THE CONTEST

the bout temporarily for any purpose, whereupon the Timekeeper stops his watch and restarts it when the fighting is resumed. Like all other officials the Timekeeper has to make sure that he has a properly-marked programme, so that he knows the length of each contest as they come up, also the duration of each round. It is also imperative that the Timekeeper calls 'Seconds Out' just prior to striking the bell or gong to denote the starting of a contest or a round. He sometimes calls 'Last Round' when such is the case.

When there is a knockdown, he not only calls out the seconds numerically, but beats with his hand on the edge of the canvas to further emphasise the count. While the count is proceeding he holds his second stop-watch in his hand, which he has picked up and started as the boxer has gone down and which he stops when the fallen man stands up. Of course, he cannot look at his watch while he is counting, his eyes having to be on both the Referee and the boxer, first to see that the Referee had taken up the count correctly, and then to watch the boxer until he rises to continue the contest. Thus, all Timekeepers must know how to count out ten seconds perfectly in order to avoid a fast or a slow count, or be in front of the Referee or behind him in the counting. A usual method of counting is to make a pause between each number by joining them with the word 'and', i.e. One-and -two-and-three-and, etc. The Timekeeper stops when he reaches 'ten', but the Referee calls 'Out' instead of 'ten' and signifies by spreading his hands that the boxer has been counted out and that the contest is over. As soon as the referee has signalled that the boxer has been counted 'out', the Timekeeper stops his other watch so that he can say at precisely what time (in minutes and seconds) the contest has ended and inform the ringside pressmen accordingly. In America the Announcer usually imparts this information to the spectators when giving them the official outcome of the contest.

Close co-operation between Timekeeper and Referee are essential if a contest is to have a satisfactory outcome that sends the fans home happy that justice has been done, even if their own particular fancy has suffered defeat. I remember a contest in New York's Madison Square Garden in 1931 when Max Baer (then on his way to the top) was matched with Tom Heeney, that heroic New Zealander, who had made a gallant but futile attempt to take the heavyweight championship from talented Gene Tunney. Jack Dempsey, former titleholder, was making his debut as a referee. In the third round, Baer pushed his rival to the ropes with such ferocity that Heeney was pushed through them. He scrambled back into the ring, but to regain his composure, dropped to one knee, whereupon Dempsey started to count.

He had reached 'eight' when Heeney got up, so the referee made the customary gesture for them to 'Box on'. This did not suit Timekeeper Arthur Donovan, however. He rang his bell to attract the attention of the referee, who held up his hand to restrain the boxers from continuing the contest and then went over to the ringside to speak to the timekeeper.

"The fight's over," Donovan told him. "I've counted out Heeney."

"But he was down only for eight seconds," said Dempsey. "How could you count him out?"

"I started my count when he was knocked out of the ring," explained the timekeeper. "When your count reached 'eight', I had got to 'ten', so the fight is over and Heeney is the loser."

Dempsey argued that the New Zealander's flight through the ropes had been the result of a shove and not a punch and that his counting was correct. It was stalemate, with both officials adamant, the boxers perplexed and the crowd yelling for action. Finally, Dempsey raised Baer's hand as the winner, thus rendering a highly controversial and unsatisfactory decision.

Provision at the ringside, or close by, for the accommodation of the Board of Control Inspector, other referees who may be awaiting their turn to officiate, and for the Announcer, who must be alert and ready to enter the ring the moment it is necessary for him to do so. Close observance of what is going on is an essential part of the Inspector's duties during a contest, to watch the lacing on of the gloves and to see that a Second does not give a stimulant of any nature to a boxer, either before or during a bout and to see that no illegal practice is attempted either knowingly, or in the case of a foreigner, in ignorance of the stipulations prevailing in the country which he is visiting. The Inspector has full power to confiscate any substance or appliance which he believes are being used illegally in either corner.

The Referee

From the spectators' point of view, the most important person in a boxing contest, apart from the two antagonists, is the referee, sometimes known as the Third Man in the ring. He is in there wide open to every form of criticism, even abuse, if the way he handles a contest or the decision he renders at the finish does not meet with

the approval of the fans, many of whom do not consider they have had their money's worth if they cannot get in the occasional 'boo' during the evening. If they feel that justice has not been done they can howl the place down and vow never to pay to see another fight, but it is all part of the beauty of Boxing and they clamour for tickets just as eagerly the next time.

Football referees, tennis umpires and judges in all forms of sport incur the disfavour of the fans at times, but disagreement with an official's action is emphasised far more when concentrated in the confines of the small area of a ring. Some men, however, enjoy being the focal point of dispute in a public entertainment and to share the limelight with the performers. This is why the majority of referees are ex-boxers. It brings them back into the limelight again. Others, who may never have pulled on a glove in combat, are equally attracted to the colourful atmosphere that Boxing provides and think the risk of being booed full compensation for the power they assume in controlling a fistic battle before a sea of eager faces.

Referees must have a full knowledge of the Rules of Boxing and the interpretation of them by the controlling body by whom they are licensed. A stiff oral examination before a special Referee's Committee, plus try-outs in the ring without rendering a verdict (this being given by a licenced referee at the ringside), must be passed before acceptance as a referee. The initial licence, known as Class 'B', (£7.50 per annum) is issued to a beginner who

It is the duty of a referee to stop a contest to avoid a boxer from taking unnecessary punishment.

THE CONTEST

can only officiate over contests of 24 minutes of actual boxing. If, however, after three years of refereeing, he does not satisfy the Referee's Committee of his ability to be up-graded to Class 'A', he may have his licence withdrawn. A Class 'A' referee can control all contests, including those covering Area Championships, or eliminating bouts for championship titles. The highest grade of Referee in Great Britain is known as Class 'A' Star and he can be appointed to take charge of any contest anywhere.

Naturally the pay differs according to the cost of the programme and how many bouts are refereed by one man at one tournament. For refereeing a whole programme costing up to £500, a 'B' official receives £15. For a thousand pounds programme, the Class 'A' referee is paid £15 for the main event(s), while the 'B' man, who takes charge of the balance of the show is entitled to £10. In the event of the programme not exceeding three scheduled bouts, one Class 'A' referee may be appointed, his fee being £20. For programmes costing up to £2,500, the 'A' referee gets £20 and the 'B' man, who officiates over the rest of the show, gets £15. For tournaments that cost up to five thousand pounds, the Board of Control remunerates the 'A' referee for the main events, the 'B' official, who covers the remainder of the programme, receiving £17.50.

Over £5,000 shows, the Board pays the 'A' referee covering the main event; the second 'A' man gets £35, and the 'B' referee, £20. When a show is televised and the programme exceeds £2,500, the referee officiating in the main televised bout is entitled to receive not less than £30. Referees who have to travel any distance, or stay overnight, are entitled to claim reasonable expenses, but it can be seen from these figures that a referee carries out his work more for love than money and sometimes it can prove a hard night's work in both a mental and physical extent.

The fees to officials quoted under the British Boxing Board of Control are the lowest allowable, but not binding. They are probably the least in most European countries where higher fees can be demanded. Also American fees would be considerably higher and vary from state to state. A manager's and boxer's licence would be based on the economy of each country's Federation expenses. In Britain the B.B.B. of C.

runs very economically because so many of its officials are unpaid, particularly the Stewards, only the General Secretary and the small office staff receive salaries. There is no limit to what a referee can be paid. Here are some examples: Ted Broadribb was paid £250 for officiating at the Young Stribling v. Primo Carnera contest at the Albert Hall in 1929, while Teddy Waltham (then General Secretary to the B.B.B. of C.) received $1,000 plus expenses to superintend the world bantam title bout between Robert Cohen and Chamrern Songkitrat at Bangkok in 1954. Largest fee of 10,000 dollars (including expenses) was paid to Jack Dempsey for refereeing the world middleweight title bout between Ceferino Garcia and Glen Lee in Manilla. He received an identical sum for being Third Man in a ten rounds non-title bout between Sixto Escobar and Simon Chavez at Caracas in Venezuela. George Blake was paid $2,500 for refereeing a match between Young Stribling and Max Schmeling at Cleveland, Ohio, in 1931 and Dempsey received a similar amount for officiating at the Rex Layne v. Ezzard Charles contest in Ogden, Utah in 1952. Nat Fleischer, editor of *The Ring* magazine was paid $1,200 (plus a thousand dollars expenses) to referee the Simon Chavez v. Joey Archibald contest in Caracas and a similar sum for the Gus Lesnevich v. Joe Kahut bout in Portland, Oregon in 1946. In Australia, Harold Valan was paid a thousand dollars (U.S.A.) to referee the world flyweight title contest between Rocky Gattellari v. Salvatore Burruni at Sydney in 1965. Since the advent of T.V., however, referee's fees have rocketed astronomically in accordance with the huge purses paid to prominent boxers–such as Muhammad Ali.

Before going into details about the duties and requirements of a modern referee, it is necessary to point out that only in Britain and some of the British Commonwealth countries, is he the sole person who renders a decision at the end of a contest. In all other countries there are judges. In the United States of America, Mexico and South America, the referee has the 'assistance' of two, situated on opposite sides of the ring, who use score cards, as does the Third Man, and the verdict is either a 'unanimous' or 'majority' decision. In Europe, however, the practice is to have three judges to name

the winner, the referee having no vote and being in the ring only to control the boxers and to see to the observance of the rules. As in international amateur boxing, the referee renders warnings that are made known to the judges by holding up both arms and making a gesture towards the side of the ring where each is sitting.

The European Boxing Union referee can end a bout by (a) counting out a fallen boxer, (b) stopping a contest that has in his view become too one-sided to warrant its continuation, (c) ending a bout after three 'standing counts' of eight seconds each that occur in one round, the 'standing count' being given after a temporary knockdown or when a boxer has received a particularly hard blow that has staggered or dazed him. The referee can also finish a contest if one of the contestants suffers a facial wound, especially in the region of the eyes, when he feels that the injury could be worsened or be detrimental to the boxer if subjected to further punching. In addition, he has the right to accept the retirement of a boxer if he is satisfied that same is justified because of the inability of the boxer to continue. 'Standing Counts' are not permitted by the B.B.B. of C., except when European title bouts take place in Great Britain, when they are fought under E.B.U. rules.

Outside Britain the theory exists that too much responsibility is placed on one man when the referee is the sole judge of the outcome of a contest. But the British fight fan has been brought up to accept a referee's decision, what is more, to regard it as final. The judges system was tried out for a time by the National Sporting Club at its headquarters in Covent Garden, London, but controversial verdicts happened just as often when three men were making a decision so the practice was abandoned. Also, the referee at the N.S.C. always sat next to the timekeeper and controlled the contest from the ringside, stopping the contest and calling the boxers up to the ropes for a caution to be administered when he thought that one or the other, or both, were guilty of transgressing the rules. This policy of having the referee outside the ropes was quite satisfactory in the small confines of an exclusive club or in the minor boxing

When a man is down the referee must keep his eye on the timekeeper, the boxer he has sent to a neutral corner and at the same time the man he is counting out.

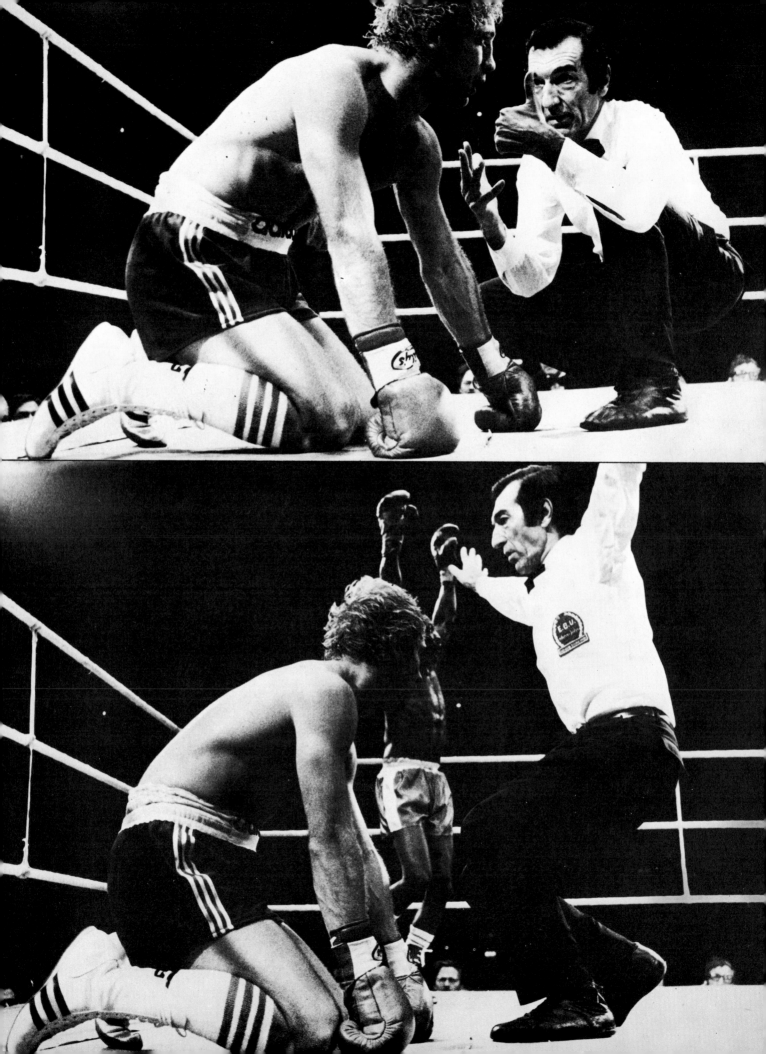

THE CONTEST

halls, but as soon as the commercial promoters appeared soon after the turn of the century, using arenas that could accommodate thousands of spectators, it was soon proved essential, from every standpoint, for the referee to be in with the boxers, a practice that has become universal.

Apart from controlling a contest and rendering his decision as to the winner, either during or at the scheduled ending, the referee must also keep his eye on the Seconds in each corner to see that the rules are being observed and to act calmly in the case of a knockdown, making sure that he takes up the count with the timekeeper at the earliest possible moment. Former world heavyweight king, Jersey Joe Walcott failed to do this when he was refereeing the return fight between Muhammad Ali and Sonny Liston at Lewiston, Maine, U.S.A. in 1965. As soon as he had put Liston down, the champion stood threateningly over his fallen rival, refusing to go to a neutral corner, whereupon Walcott tried to move him away by force. By the time he got round to taking up the count and went over to the timekeeper to do so, he found that twenty seconds had elapsed and he was told that Liston had been counted out, not once, but twice by the man with the watch, and when Walcott returned to the centre of the ring to acclaim Ali as the winner, he found that Liston was on his feet and

the fight was being continued. It was a complete shambles.

All in all a referee has plenty on his hands and must vary his actions to meet each situation as it arises. He may have two upstanding boxers who are easy to control, or a pair who want to indulge in a free-for-all scrimmage. Flyweights provide an entirely different type of contest from heavies; when 'southpaw' boxers are involved there is a natural variation in moves and punches that must be watched. The referee who does his job efficiently needs a strong personality and an alert and determined mind. He must have a practical knowledge of the rules which must be strictly interpreted with honesty, impartiality and commonsense. Ex-boxers, especially champions, do not necessarily make the best referees as they are apt to judge more favourably men who have a similar style to the one they employed in their salad days.

Referees must not be swayed by sentimentality, by creed or by colour. Impartiality does not come easy to the human mind, more especially in the excited atmosphere of a boxing arena and the tense battle of brain and brawn in a small area surrounded by thousands who have paid for and are entitled to give fair vent to the feelings

When in charge of novices the referee must stamp his authority on the contest from the start.

and partisanship. Even with a strict observance of the rules, there are times when the referee must use his discretionary powers with promptness and justice. When he is called upon to act, he is the sole decider, there being no time or opportunity to consult others.

He must have the utmost confidence in his judgment without being dictatorial and be deaf to the roar of the crowd. He must not baulk from naming a man as a winner if by so doing he incurs the wrath of the onlookers. If he feels it is necessary to disqualify a boxer he must do so unhesitatingly and with firmness. He must be prepared for the unexpected and meet it with expedition and determination. Throughout a contest he must let the audience and the boxers know that he, and he alone, is in complete control. By his handling of a bout he must earn the respect of both contestants as well as the spectators, but whilst emphasising his authority, the referee must remain obscure and do nothing to draw attention to himself during the actual exchanges. Over zealous Referees and those who want to be 'in on the act' can ruin a contest, just as a quiet, cool and efficient Third Man can make one into an epic and memorable bout.

Obviously it is essential for a referee to be physically and mentally fit. A fifteen rounds contest, if it goes the scheduled distance, can keep a man on his feet under the heat of powerful arc lights for a full hour and during the actual rounds of fighting he must be on the move all the time, not only to observe what is going on between the boxers, but also to keep out of the vision of the fans. He has to be watching the exchanges from every angle to keep pace with the fast-moving opponents. More than once I have seen a highly efficient referee working-out in a boxing gymnasium to prepare himself physically for a forthcoming bout that promises plenty of strenuous activity on his part. I recall that Eugene Corri, one of England's most notable referees, took himself off for a week's training before officiating at the Mickey Walker *v.* Tommy Milligan fight for the world's middleweight championship at Olympia, London, in 1927. He knew it would be a lively contest that was scheduled for twenty rounds and he wanted to make sure he could last out this marathon battle which, as it happened, ended in a knockout win for Walker in the tenth.

In the Ring

As soon as he has been introduced, the Referee beckons both men to the centre of the ring and gives them a short discourse on what he expects from them. He probably says: "You both know the rules. I expect you to abide by them. Shake hands and come out fighting." American referees usually have a lot more to say and they use a microphone so that the fans can hear what is said to the fighters. Famous referee Ruby Goldstein had this to say when he refereed the return fight between Sugar Ray Robinson and Randolph Turpin in New York in 1951. "When there's a knockdown, I want the other fellow to go right back to the farthest neutral corner without hesitation. If you don't you'll only be wasting time, because I shall not take up the count until my orders are obeyed. You can hit in the clinches provided you have one hand free, but if you've not, then I shall break you up. May the better man win." If, however, the boxers are in the early stages of their careers a referee will impress on them that when ordered to 'break' from a clinch they should do so immediately; that they must defend themselves at all times; punch only with the knuckle part of a closed glove; retire to the farthest neutral corner in the event of a knockdown, and not to renew the contest until ordered to do so. When giving these instructions the Referee should examine the faces and bodies of the contestants for signs of any superfluous greasing. If he sees any, he sends the boxer back to his corner to have it removed.

When the Referee has returned the fighters to their respective corners, he glances at the Timekeeper to show he is ready for the contest to start. The Timekeeper calls 'Seconds Out' and clangs his gong and it is up to the Referee to see that the ring is clear of everyone, except the two boxers and himself, then he motions them together for the commencement of the exchanges. In America and some other countries they blow a whistle to clear the ring ten seconds before the gong or bell is sounded to start the contest. Once the bout has commenced, the referee must not permit any shouting or signalling to a boxer from those in his corner, indeed he has the power to stop the contest and issue a warning to those responsible. If this is ignored he can order the offender out of the corner for the remainder of the contest.

For a considerable time in the early days of glove-fighting the entry of a Second into the ring during a contest would cause the instant disqualification of his boxer and bouts were sometimes brought to an abrupt conclusion by this means. When that redoubtable Scottish flyweight, Benny Lynch, was champion, he was saved from almost certain knockout defeat by this means, his chief Second, Nick Cavalli, jumping into the ring after Lynch had been put down for a long count by Len Hampston from Batley in Yorkshire. Benny was immediately disqualified, but it was considered less a blot on his record to have been ruled out rather than be knocked out. Nowadays, if a Second gets into the ring during a knockdown, the Referee keeps him away from the fallen boxer and proceeds with the count. If he reaches the 'out' he signals the end of the contest, but if the boxer gets up in time to beat the count, the bout is stopped and the offending Second ordered out of the ring and out of the corner, and is then subject to subsequent disciplinary action by his Area Council.

In the past a Second could end a contest by throwing in a towel, but the modern Referee ignores such a gesture, it being in *his* hands to decide when a boxer should be retired from a contest. If a Referee thinks it necessary, he can go to a corner and examine a boxer who may have taken heavy punishment or been put down during a round or suffered a cut around the eyes that has caused bleeding. He can consult the manager and seconds, even the boxer himself, and if he is satisfied that the bout should be stopped in the boxer's interests, he has the power to do so. On the other hand, those in a corner can call over a Referee if they feel their man has had enough and ask for permission to retire him. But it is up to the Referee to make the final decision.

In the event of a glove bursting during a bout, the Referee must stop the contest instruct the Timekeeper to take time off, order the boxers to the two neutral corners and send for a replacement glove – promoters are required to have a spare pair available for just such an emergency. The boxer with the damaged glove should then go to his corner and the change made as quickly as possible under the supervision of the Referee. If, however, the burst is of quite a minor character and not likely to expose the wearer or his opponent to any danger, the contest may be allowed to continue until the end of the round and the change effected during the interval period between the rounds.

Smart seconds have been known to use delaying tactics when their boxer has been badly hurt by interfering with a glove during an interval. There was the highly suspect case of Angelo Dundee, chief second to Cassius Clay (as he was then known) in the first fight with Henry Cooper at Wembley Stadium in 1963. Just before the end of the fourth round the Britisher put his American opponent down with his celebrated left hook to the chin and Clay was in a badly dazed condition when the bell to end the round came to his rescue. In the corner it was discovered that one of Clay's gloves had burst open to expose his bare fist and some time was wasted while this state of affairs was hotly debated between Dundee, the referee and the Board of Control officials at the ringside. Meanwhile Clay was restored to such efficiency that he was able to stop Cooper in the next round.

Of course, the Referee has to keep his eye on both corners to see that nothing untoward is taking place, i.e. the damaging of a glove, the application of excess vaseline on the face or the giving of any stimulant other than cold water. He takes it all in while standing in a neutral corner during the interval between the rounds marking his score card. As soon as the Timekeeper calls 'Seconds Out', he goes into the centre of the ring and awaits the arrival of the boxers from their corners to continue the contest.

Points scoring, like refereeing, varies in different parts of the world. If a boxer fights in a foreign country, he must abide by the rules that exist there; similarly if a British boxer fights for or in defence of an European championship, he must do so under European Boxing Union rules. even if he does so in his own country, where the rules vary from those of the E.B.U.

THE BIG FIGHT

This pictorial sequence of a championship contest depicts typical incidents and how fortunes can change during the course of a bout. Many fans who disagree with a referee's verdict are apt to forget what has happened in the early rounds and this 'strip fight' gives you the whole picture.

THE CROWD IS TENSE AS THE CHAMPION ENTERS THE RING... HIS ORTHODOX BOXING SHOULD BE TOO MUCH FOR THE NON-STOP AGGRESSION OF THE YOUNG

ROUND 2

THE CHAMPION SETTLES DOWN USING THE STRAIGHT LEFT TO GOOD ADVANTAGE... KEEPING HIS OPPONENT AT BAY THE CHAMPION TOOK THAT BY A CLEAR MARGIN...

IT'S ABOVE THE RIGHT EYE!

IT'S A BAD ONE

WATCH YOUR HEAD!

HE MUST BOX HIM...

ROUND 3

HE'S GOT T

THE CHALLENGER PULLS BACK WITH BLOOD SEEPING FROM A CUT...THE BELL! THE ROUND WAS EVE

HALLENGER THE BELL!

THE CHAMPION MISSES WITH A WILD SWING...

UND 2 AND THE CHAMP IS CAUGHT A RIGHT CROSS... HE'S DOWN...

3...4...5 UP ON HIS KNEES... SAVED BY THE BELL... HE'S CUT...

USE HIS LEFT... THE CHAMP IS FIGHTING BACK...LEFT...LEFT...THERE'S A CLASH OF HEADS!

THIS COULD BE THE TURNING POINT... THE CHALLENGER LOOKS DISPIRITED

THE CONTEST

In Prize Ring days, contests were fought to a finish, the referee's task being to see that the rounds (which ended in a knockdown or fall and had no time schedule) were fairly fought and to render a decision at the finish. In the early days of glove-fighting, so-called 'Fights to a Finish' were usually advertised as for 45 rounds. Later the limit was restricted to 20 rounds and eventually reduced to fifteen.

In Britain contests were decided on a points basis, with a maximum of five to each round to the winner of the round in the referee's estimation, and a fraction of five to the loser, i.e. $4\frac{3}{4}$ if it had been fairly close, $4\frac{1}{2}$ if the difference was wider (if the loser had been put down for a count or been subjected to heavy punishment). A wider difference would indicate that the bout should be stopped because of the undoubted superiority of one boxer over the other. When Freddie Welsh, from Wales, fought Willie Ritchie, of America, for the latter's world lightweight title at Olympia, London, in 1914, Referee Eugene Corri made the Welshman the winner and new champion by a mere quarter of a point.

The European countries that took up Boxing from Britain, followed the British style of points scoring for a time, but later used a maximum of ten points and without fractions. The British Boxing Board of Control adopted this method until 1977, but using half-points to make a closer definition. To try and keep in line with the rest of Europe in the matter of judging contests, it has, however, followed suit and all professional contests now have a maximum of ten points, with any differences confined to whole points, i.e. 10–9, 10–8, etc.

In America the points scoring varies almost from State to State as each has its separate Boxing Commission, and while some are members of the World Boxing Council others are members of the rival World Boxing Association. With the New York State Commission, which cannot legally attach itself to any other body, the judges and referees assess a contest on both round-by-round scoring *and* points scoring. If a bout ends in a 'draw', so far as rounds scored are concerned, then the winner is based on the points score. This is how the system works: One point is scored for the boxer winning the round by a shade, nothing for the loser. When the round is a clear win, two points are credited to the winner and

none for the loser. If it is a one-sided round, the winner receives three points and the loser none. Three points are also awarded if a boxer scores a knockdown and is well out in front. If it is a one-sided round, plus more than one knock-down, the winner is allotted four points.

In the majority of the States that are members of the World Boxing Association, the five points system is used. In this, the winner of the round receives the maximum and the loser gets four. A positive knockdown with a clear margin for the round, gives the winner a clear 5–3 advantage with the margin becoming wider. In Massachusetts, Ohio, Texas and Miami, the ten points system is used. New Jersey uses the rounds method, while in California the five points system prevails, under which the winner of a round can earn anything from 1 to 5 points, while the loser receives none. An even round is scored 0–0. All other countries where pro Boxing is practiced, outside Europe and the United States, have their own interpretation of the way a Boxing contest should be judged and the winner decided, but in general they follow the systems as used by the majority of the American Boxing Commissions.

As the Noble Art of Self Defence emanated in Britain, the methods of scoring as laid down by the British Boxing Board of Control, which have been perfected by time, appear fair and adequate. John Broughton laid down the original rules for Prize Fighting in 1743 and these remained unaltered until 1838 when they were amended by the British Pugilists' Protective Association, who introduced the London Prize Ring Rules or the New Rules of Prize Fighting. They were revised in 1853 and again in 1866, but a year later the 8th Marquess of Queensberry introduced an entirely fresh set of rules in which it was compulsory to wear gloves. These were universally accepted. Modifications were made and published by *The Sporting Life*, a daily paper devoted to Horse Racing, but having a great influence in Boxing circles. These were further amended by the National Sporting Club in 1909 and again in 1923. They were adopted by the British Boxing Board of Control, which brought them up-to-date when it was re-constituted in 1929 and has maintained and amended them to meet the times ever since. They are uncompli-

cated and easily understood by both the fighting men and referees.

Each referee receives a Score Card as he enters the ring to control a contest. It is a simple affair (see illustration) and he marks it up before the bout begins with the name of each boxer, the colour of their trunks, the date, the venue, the name of the promotor and the number of rounds to be contested. After each round he retires to a neutral corner and enters the points he has awarded each boxer. There is a column in which he can mark the advantage one man has over the other, also one in which he can keep a total of the marks scored by each boxer round by round, thus enabling him to tell quickly which man has secured most points and is therefore the winner of the contest. If a boxer is counted out or the referee stops the bout because it has become one-sided, or disqualifies him for a breach of the rules, he receives no points for that round and consequently loses the contest as the referee awards his opponent maximum points for that round. The last column on the card is for 'Remarks' in which he enters the time of each knockdown, also any cautions or warnings he has had to deliver during the course of the round. At the foot of the card he writes the actual result, i.e. Smith counted out in 11th round, or Robinson retired, stopped or disqualified in 5th round; or Jones won on points. If the total on each side of the card is equal then he writes the word 'draw' to indicate that the scores are level.

It would be well at this juncture to explain why and how the term 'draw', denoting that one side is equal to the other, came about. For the best part of every year millions of people try to forecast drawn results in Football without realising the origin of the term. In all forms of racing it is known as a 'dead heat', but for the 'draw' we must again return to the Prize Ring. When it was found necessary to stake out a square for the fighting men, those who wanted to back a boxer or put up the money for their particular fancy, tied their purses to the post in that particular corner, thus providing the 'stakes', a word that nowadays denotes the prize money to be won or a wager. If darkness fell making it impossible for the fight to continue, or the crowd broke into the ring, or the police appeared, or neither man could come out from his corner through

The referees score card tells the complete story, round by round.

exhaustion, or the contestants shook hands and refused to fight any more, the referee pulled up the stakes to indicate that the affair was over with neither man the winner. He 'drew' the stakes or ordered them to be with-drawn from the ground. The official result was therefore a 'draw'.

The B.B.B. of C. Rules say that marks shall be awarded for 'attack' – direct clean hits with the knuckle part of the glove of either hand on any part of the front or sides of the head or body above the belt, an imaginary line drawn across the body from the top of the hip bones; for 'defence' – guarding, slipping, ducking or getting away from an opponent's punches. When boxers are otherwise equal, the majority of the marks are given to the one who does most of the leading or displays the better style.

It is no easy matter for a referee to decide and retain in his mind all the exchanges that transpire over a period of three minutes fought at top speed. But he learns to do this and must not be influenced by the boxer who restrains himself in the first two minutes of each round and then makes an all-out assault in the remaining sixty seconds in order to catch the official eye and influence the spectators, who are apt to forget what has occurred in the early part of the round.

Quality rather than quantity is what the referee must look for and he must also watch for effectiveness in both attack and defence. Footwork, style, and ring generalship must also be noted and while there is a saying that attack is the best form of defence, a boxer can be entirely on the defensive for a whole round and yet pick up the majority of the points, in fact, what is known as 'milling on the retreat' can be brought to a fine art and have match-winning qualities. If a referee has a boxer ten marks in front of his opponent he must automatically stop the contest as obviously there is no possibility of him catching up, except by scoring a knockout, in which case the result would be a farcical 'draw'.

Although the word 'knockout' is generally accepted, as the decisive ending to a bout, the correct term is 'count out', in other words, the boxer is counted out of the time allowed for him to get to his feet and continue the contest, i.e. ten seconds. The reason why all contests in Britain are decided on points, irrespective of whether they finish inside the scheduled distance, is to satisfy the law and signifies the distinction between Boxing and Prize-Fighting, the latter being illegal. The sport has never in fact been legalised in Britain, but by using the word 'contest' instead of 'fight', 'boxer'

REFEREE'S SCORE SHEET 3

Date 1. JAN 1975   No. of Rounds 15
Promoter C. GREENE
Venue THE STADIUM
Referee TOM SMITH
(WHITE TRUNKS) BROWN v. JONES (RED TRUNKS)

Total Marks	Advantage	Score	Round	Score	Advantage	Total Marks	Remarks
		10	1	10			
	1	10	2	9½			
	1	10	3	9½			
		10	4	10			B.y.4.
		9	5	10	2		
		9½	6	10	1		
		9½	7	10	1		
		10	8	10			J.C.L.B
	1	10	9	9½			
		9½	10	10	1		
		0	11	10			
			12			108½	
97½							
		BROWN COUNTED OUT	14	11th ROUND			
			15				

THE CONTEST

instead of 'fighter', dispensing with the term 'knockout', and having the professional side governed by a properly constituted Board of Control it is allowable as a form of public entertainment.

We have already seen the duties of the Timekeeper in the event of a knockdown and the Referee's actions must coincide with these. As soon as a boxer goes down, he must send his opponent to the farthest neutral corner, then move into a position close to the fallen man, take up the count from the Timekeeper and call out the seconds, waving his hand downwards to give a dazed boxer every opportunity to understand how long he has been on the canvas. As soon as the man gets to his feet, he should wipe any dust from his gloves, look carefully and quickly into the eyes to see that he is capable of continuing the contest, then motion the men together and order them to 'Box On'. If he reaches 'nine' and 'out', he spreads his arms wide to signify that the contest is over and walks over to the other man and raises his arm to signify that he is the winner. He can do this if the contest has gone the full distance in order to render his verdict, then he must inform the Announcer when that official gets into the ring, by what margin of points he has come to his decision and on leaving the ring himself, hand his completed and signed score card to the Board of Control Inspector – and no one else.

Some fans are mystified when a man is declared to have been counted out when he is in the act of rising. If the boxer is still completely on the floor when the count reaches 'nine' and then starts to get up, it is obvious that he will not be on his feet and in a position to defend himself before the 'out' is called. On the other hand, if he is resting on one knee at the count of 'nine', then rises immediately and puts up his hands, he will have beaten the count, if only by a split second. A man is considered 'down', even if he is on one foot or both feet while at the same time any other part of his body is touching the floor of the ring, in which case the referee is fully entitled to start counting in unison with the Time-keeper.

Should the count be interrupted by the bell sounding to end the round, the referee continues counting and if he reaches the 'out' the contest is over. If, however, the boxer manages to get to his feet before the 'out' is called, he can return to his corner and be entitled to continue the contest, in other words, he has been 'saved by the bell'. Before this important rule was introduced, it was possible and happened many times, that an unconscious boxer was picked up by his seconds, carried to his stool or chair when frantic attempts were made to revive him sufficiently so that he could be sent up for another round. Far too often he was in no condition to take another punch, despite the strenuous efforts of his handlers and consequently was in danger of receiving a blow that could be very dangerous, even lethal. Up to the Second World War it was a common practice of Seconds to hold a dazed man on his seat, slap his face, twist his ears and spray water over him in order to restore him to consciousness. Happily all these primitive methods of first aid in the corner have now been vetoed.

On those rare occasions where both boxers have been put to the boards at the same time, the count proceeds in the normal way, and if one gets up but the other is unable to do so before the count out, then the first one on his feet is automatically the winner. If, however, both men are counted out, the boxer who was ahead on points at the end of the last completed round, according to the Referee's score card, is declared the winner. Should a simultaneous count out occur in the opening round of the contest, then the result is declared a 'draw'. Should a boxer be put to the canvas, rises during the count, then drops again, the Referee must first satisfy himself that the boxer has fallen the second time from the effects of the punch that originally dropped him and not gone down to avoid a follow-up punch or to take a few more seconds in which to recover, and either rule out the boxer for going down without taking a punch or continue the count from the point at which it was interrupted and go on until either the boxer gets up or is counted out.

A contest should never be stopped whilst the count is proceeding, except in a case where the Referee feels that the fallen man is in need of immediate medical aid. Should a felled boxer rise in time to beat the count, but is in no condition to defend himself, either mentally or physically, the contest must be brought to an immediate conclusion by the Referee. If a boxer has been counted out and remains on the floor of the ring in an unconscious state, it is the duty of the Referee to see that he remains unmoved by his Seconds until the ringside doctor is in attendance, when they obey his instructions. To aid the boxer, the Referee should turn his head to one side and remove his gum-shield, a procedure to prevent the stricken man from the danger of choking. The boxer is allowed to remain inert until the doctor thinks it safe for him to be helped to his corner when he supervises his restoration to full consciousness. If he cannot be revived to enable him to leave the ring unaided, then the doctor orders his removal on a stretcher to the dressing-room where he renders further aid and, if he considers it necessary, has an ambulance sent for and the boxer taken to hospital. It is the duty of every promoter to make sure that a stretcher is kept within easy reach under the ring.

According to most Rules of the Boxing Authorities the world over, the Referee has the power to disqualify a contestant for any of the following acts: (a) hitting below the 'belt' line; (b) using the pivot blow (a back-hand swing from either hand); (c) hitting on the back of the head or neck (known as the 'rabbit' punch for obvious reasons; and (d) punching to the kidney region of the body. Fouls can also be committed by (e) hitting with the open glove, the inside or butt of the glove, or with the wrist or elbow; (f) excessive holding, butting or careless use of the head; (g) for not trying; (h) persistently ducking below the waist line; (i) intentional falling without receiving a blow; (j) failing to 'break' when so ordered or striking, or attempting to strike, an opponent on the 'break'; (k) deliberately striking an opponent when he is dropping to the floor or when he is actually down; (l) for ungentlemanly conduct; (m) for any act or misconduct which the referee considers foul.

As intimated in the chapter devoted to 'The Boxer', any man who is disqualified from a contest by a referee is automatically brought before his Area Council when his case is considered and if found guilty he can be severely cautioned or fined according to the nature of his misconduct. He may appeal for a re-hearing by the Area Council or for his case to be heard by the Stewards of Appeal, but must first place a deposit of £5. with the Board of Control which he forfeits if his appeal is rejected.

The Care of the Boxer

It is imperative that the utmost care is taken of the boxer whether he be an amateur or a professional, not only for humanity's sake, but to keep him in the sport as a fit competitor for as long as possible – or as long as he keeps his 'silk' or physical perfection. To shorten this limited period of his career by neglect or mishandling is to reduce the number of active boxers, which is naturally against the interests of all those connected with the sport. In the dark days of the Fight Game, when boxers were ten a penny, or a dime a dozen as they said in America, such care over a boxer's destiny was regrettably not so urgent, but the modern controlling body does everything to ensure that there is no wastage of talent through mismanagement or that any boy who takes up boxing is allowed to suffer any permanent injury or the after effects of a fistic career. The one-time term of 'punch-drunkenness', or mental and physical deterioration through the excessive absorbtion of punches, is now happily a thing of the past, every effort being taken to see that it is avoided.

Again I take the British Board of Control's regulations, not only as a general guide to what transpires elsewhere in the world of Boxing, but also because they cannot be excelled anywhere. For instance, Boxers over 18 but under 19 years of age are not permitted to engage in contests of more than 24 minutes of actual boxing (8 × 3), while those over 19 but under 20 must not take part in bouts that last more than 30 minutes of actual boxing, i.e. ten rounds of three minutes each round. While no boxer is granted a professional licence under the age of 18, an enthusiastic boy of 17 can obtain an 'Apprentice-Professional' licence which permits him to participate in contests not exceeding eight minutes of boxing, i.e. four rounds of two minutes each round.

No boxer is allowed to take part in a contest within four clear days from the date of his last bout, or in a main event or chief contest within six clear days of his last bout; what constitutes a Chief Contest being the prerogative of his Area Council to decide. The controlling body does, however, reserve the right to waive this regulation, but only when a substitute is required and when the boxer concerned has won his first bout within two rounds. The days when a fighter could go through a contest and then return to the ring for another bout during the course of one programme are fortunately gone for ever. Nor can a boxer fight at one hall and then proceed to another for a contest on the same day.

When a contest is stopped by the Referee because one man is outclassed or has suffered a nasty cut, particularly in the region of the eyes, or by the retirement of the boxer, or by a 'knockout', the licence of the loser is automatically suspended for a period of at least 21 days thereafter and is not restored until he is certified as fit to box by a doctor who may be appointed by the Board of Control or his Area Council, such written certificate to be received at Head Office at least 24 hours prior to the boxer's next contest. Any boxer losing four consecutive contests may be suspended until he appears before his Area Council for investigation, at which the attendance of his manager may also be requested. No boxer who is under suspension may act as a sparring-partner to another boxer, or appear in an exhibition bout, while similarly, no licenced boxer may engage a suspended boxer as a spar-mate. Every boxer must be medically examined annually in accordance with the Board of Control medical form,

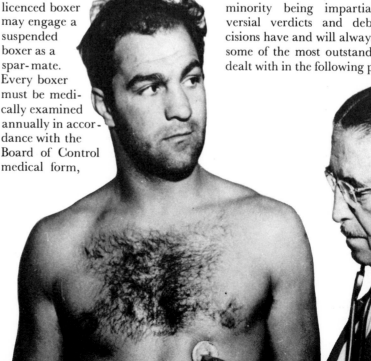

when his licence is due for renewal.

All doctors who are engaged at boxing shows must be appointed by the Board of Control. They attend tournaments on a rota basis at such places as are most convenient to themselves. Apart from examining and passing as fit boxers at the weigh-in for contests, their duties entail the further examination of boxers in their dressing-rooms and when this duty is accomplished they proceed to the ring-side where a seat is reserved for them by the promoter. They remain in close vicinity to the ring throughout the tournament, being ready to go to the aid of a boxer as and when required. If summoned to the dressing-room because their services are requested there, it is their duty to inform the ringside Inspector where they can be found. At some major shows it has sometimes been found necessary to engage two doctors so that any emergency situation may be met.

All officials, whether acting in or out of the ring, indeed all licenced members in whatever capacity who are connected with any particular contest, are required to maintain order to the best of their ability, before, during and after the bout has ended; this for the sake of law and order, also for the good of the sport. Referees are not infallible and their methods of controlling contests and the decisions they make are always open to hostile criticism, especially in the case of an important fight when the spectators can be divided into two distinct sides, with the smallest minority being impartial. Controversial verdicts and debatable decisions have and will always occur and some of the most outstanding will be dealt with in the following pages.

BOXING SENSATIONS

1915
Top left: Jess Willard, the giant cowboy, knocking out Jack Johnson for the World Championship at Havana, Cuba.

1927
Above: Jack Dempsey (left) *v.* Gene Tunney in the famous Battle of the Long Count at Chicago, Illinois, U.S.A.

1961
Left: Emile Griffith (left) winning the world crown from Benny (Kid) Paret at New York, U.S.A. Six months later Paret regained the title, but lost it back to Griffith in a third match that caused his death.

1951

Top left: Sugar Ray Robinson *v.* Randolph Turpin in their return fight for the world crown at New York, U.S.A. Turpin won the first contest at London 64 days earlier.

1952

Above: Yoshio Shirai (right) became the first Japanese world champion by defeating Dado Marino in Tokyo, Japan.

1938

Left: Henry Armstrong (standing) made ring history by being the first boxer to hold three world titles at one and the same time. Here he is completing the hat-trick at the expense of Lou Ambers in New York, U.S.A.

BOXING SENSATIONS

1921
Top left: The first Million Dollar Gate. Heavyweight champion Jack Dempsey of America knocking out Georges Carpentier of France in the fourth round at Jersey City, N.J., U.S.A.

1930
Above: Max Schmeling (Germany) winning the vacant world heavyweight title on an alleged foul from Jack Sharkey (U.S.A.) in the fourth round at New York, U.S.A. The only case in boxing history when the heavyweight championship has been won by disqualification of one of the contestants.

1959
Left: Ingemar Johansson became the first Swede to win the world title by knocking out Floyd Patterson in three rounds at New York, U.S.A.

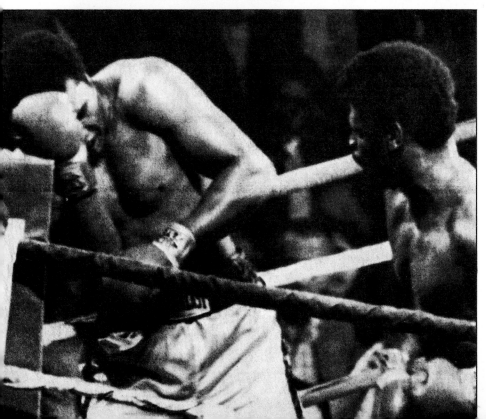

Muhammad Ali (formerly Cassius Clay) has probably caused more sensations during his career than any other boxer. The cry "I am the Greatest" brought a new dimension to the fight game. Ask anyone from New York to Singapore "Who is the Greatest?" and they will tell you Muhammad Ali.

1963
Top: Henry Cooper, British Champion, floored Cassius Clay (Muhammad Ali) in a non-title bout at London, England.

1965
Centre left: Muhammad Ali (left) a moment before putting down the champion Sonny Liston in one minute of the opening round of their heavyweight championship fight at Lewiston, Maine, U.S.A.

1971
Centre right: Muhammad Ali having been stripped of his title by the N.Y.A.C. makes a fruitless attempt to regain it from Joe Frazier.

1978
Bottom: Leon Spinks scored one of boxing's greatest upsets when he captured the world title with a 15-round split decision over Muhammad Ali. At going to press Spinks has been deprived of his title by the W.B.A. and Ken Norton recognised as champion in his stead.

THE PROMOTER

There would be no commercialised Boxing without the promoters; men prepared to find the money to pay for the staging of tournaments, to make the matches that appeal to the public and attract them to the box-office, although some promoters prefer to engage a qualified matchmaker and leave the rest to him. Most promoters, apart from the money-making aspect, are devout followers of the sport and will risk their cash to put on a fight that they particularly want to see or which involves a boxer in whom they have an especial liking. Some have themselves been boxers and take to promoting as a means of keeping in close touch with the profession and also to take an important role in its continuation. They are always looking for the likely lad they can help raise to a position in emulation of their own past successes or to attain the prominence they had once hoped to reach themselves.

All through Boxing history there have been two classes of promoters those who run the small arenas in the towns where Boxing is popular and who provide a constant supply of promising men for the larger scale promoters to exploit at the major arenas in the cities. In the 1930's there were as many as a hundred shows a week of one size or another up and down the country in Gt. Britain, with as many as twenty tournaments on a Monday night, the most popular day of the week. The same could be said of most other countries where Boxing formed part of mass entertainment, especially in the United States where there were fight towns in abundance and regular big shows in all the major cities. But the coming of the Welfare State and the raising of the standard of living in the affluent countries reduced the number of fighting men considerably and the promoters of later years have had a much harder job to fill their programmes or stage as many shows as in the past. In the same pattern, the majority of fighters now come from the so-termed under-privileged nations, while in Europe and the United States of America, competitors are on the wane.

Wherever he may be the promoter has a business that is fraught with risk and frustration. First he must find his fight, his main attraction, then he must hire a hall or book an arena in which to stage it, the size of the place being based on the number of spectators who will clamour to see it. There is also the necessity for a worthy supporting programme, four or five other bouts between men who have built up a following for themselves and can be relied upon as good ticket sellers. So he has his main event, his place in which to promote it and the supporting items, all of which take a lot of negotiation into which he must enter even if he has the assistance of a matchmaker. Apart from an office and a staff to run it, he has to consider the cost of advertising, the entertainment of the sporting press, the approval of his controlling body, the engagement of his officials and, in the event of a big show that will attract thousands, the assistance of the police in the event of a disturbance due to a disputed decision or a sensational ending in the electrifying atmosphere of a much-publicised bout.

Having finalised his preparations the promoter cannot relax until the moment when his two principals climb into their respective corners ready to do battle. There is always the risk that one or the other might break down in training or suffer an injury that forces him to seek a postponement. Jack Solomons once had an international match of the greatest importance within a few days of fulfilment when one of the boxers concerned ran a lorry into a tree and so damaged himself that the contest had to be put off for the best part of a year. There is also the possibility that an arranged contest that looks a winner on paper does not meet with sufficient appeal, in which case the promoter has the choice of cutting his losses and cancelling the show, whereupon he may have to pay compensation to the boxers involved, or to carry on and suffer financial disaster. He has constantly to refer to his ticket-selling employee to see that things are going smoothly, or whether he must increase his publicity. Sometimes, of course, there are occasions when he can cheerfully announce a sell-out, but that is not often and does not diminish the hazards to which the promoting of boxing tournaments is prone.

Like the manager, the promoter must keep himself fully aware of what is going on in the world of Boxing: must know what other promoters are doing, what progress boxers are making, the moves and decisions made by the various controlling bodies and any changes that may occur in the rules and regulations. In some instances he must have official sanction for a match, especially if he proposes to announce it as being for a championship. Of course, managers are continually coming to him pressing the claims of their boxers and, suggesting attractive matches, all of which helps, but he has to be able to judge the true merits of each case and not be swayed by argument or sentiment. He must also be aware of the earning power of each boxer and what he can afford to pay him, also it is of inestimable value if the fighter has a local following that enables him to guarantee ticket sales that will go a long way towards the extent of his purse money.

When building up his programme the promoter must take a long-term view, planning one contest that will lead to another of more importance. He must make gentleman agreements with managers whose boxers he is cultivating so that he can call upon their services as his plans mature. Likewise

Don King from Cleveland, Ohio has lived up to his name with regard to the televising of big fights via the satellite technique.

94

ALI
V
FOREMAN

THE PROMOTER

As already stated in this book one reason for the diminishing number of tournaments held today is that there are fewer "hungry fighters" around. Another reason is the increasing cost to the promoter of staging an attractive show. One of his problems is to find a sufficient number of "ticket selling" boxers who can bring a big local following wherever they appear. Below we have attempted in very basic terms to show the narrow margins the promoter has to work to.

COSTS
Contests
2 International Non-Title Fights at 10 rounds each.
3 Non-International Fights at 8 rounds each.
1 Novice Fight at 6 rounds.
Total Purse Money — $34,000
(This may vary as some "top of the bill" boxers take a percentage)

Administration
Hire of Hall, Referees, House Seconds and other officials, Advertising, Printing and Catering etc. $16,000

TOTAL COSTS $50,000   *an Exchange Rate of $2 = £1*

REVENUE
Hall capacity : 6,000
Seats actually filled : 4,500
If the price of tickets ranges between $4.20 (Gallery) to $24 (Ringside) the average revenue per head will be $16

TOTAL REVENUE $72,000
(Minus expenses incurred during pre- tournament negotiations)

he must secure a lease on any arena that he uses periodically so that he is sure of having a venue for any important contest that might, as is quite often the case in Boxing, come out of the blue and demand instant presentation. Even after taking every precaution, his well-laid plans can come sadly adrift through circumstances entirely beyond his control, or because of the activities of a rival promoter, perhaps even one in another country.

A striking example is the time when Sydney Hulls, one of the best of London's major promoters, endeavoured to stage a fight for the heavyweight championship of the world between Max Schmeling, of Germany, and Tommy Farr, the British title-holder. James J. Braddock was the champion, but had refused to meet Schmeling in a title defence although ordered to do so by the New York State Athletic Commission. Mike Jacobs, America's leading promoter, did not want to risk having a German as world champion, this being in the Nazi era, so bribed Braddock into defending his crown against Joe Louis instead. This was a wrong thing to do from every standpoint, as Schmeling held a knockout win over Louis, and as soon as Jacobs' plan became known to Hulls, he immediately matched Farr with Schmeling and arranged to stage the fight at Cardiff, billing it as for the world title.

This step alarmed Jacobs, who feared he would lose his grip on the world heavyweight situation. So he sent an emissary to England with a blank cheque and a tempting contract that included a number of contests in America other than one for the championship. He dangled this before Farr and his manager, Ted Broadribb, who accepted the offer, leaving Promoter Hulls out in the cold. To complete the story, Braddock lost to Louis, but picked up 10 per cent of every championship purse earned by his conqueror thereafter – such was the bribe – while Farr lost to Louis, but not before he had given him the fight of his life. Tommy then lost four further contests in New York, and came home to be handsomely forgiven by Hulls who provided the Welshman with an opportunity to reverse one of his American defeats.

In Great Britain the small promoter has all but vanished and in his place has come the private sporting clubs, where the members can wine and dine before seeing an evening's programme of Boxing. These clubs are promoting bodies and appoint their own match-maker. The members pay an annual fee that covers the Boxing entertainment and they can purchase tickets for guests if they wish. To a certain extent these clubs serve as nurseries for the big promoter, but not in such rich vein as did the small public arenas of the past where the atmosphere was more inducive to keen competition and where fans living in the neighbourhood of the boxers could come and give enthusiastic local support and encouragement; where the favourites of one street could battle with those of a rival residency.

When such places as *The Ring* at Blackfriars, *Premierland* in the East End, the *Alcazar* at Edmonton, and the Public Baths halls were running regular weekly shows, London was full of young, enthusiastic and ambitious boxers encouraged to give of their best by local partisanship and most cities in the rest of the country were likewise turning out up-and-coming boys and prospective champions. Nowadays promoters have to rely on the amateur champions and near champions to fill their programmes, boxers who get into what is known as the Big Time without having had the essential apprenticeship in the more obscure arenas. They reach championship status with only a few fights under their belts with the result that with few exceptions they are not equipped to be pitted against fighters who have been welded in a tougher and more competitive field.

A Promoter's Obligations

Like everyone else connected with Boxing the promoter must hold a licence issued by his controlling body. In the case of the British Boxing Board of Control he makes his application through the Area Council that governs the area in which he wishes to operate. His qualifications to promote, his business reputation and financial standing are examined and when it is agreed that he should be given a licence he must deposit with the Board a sum of money in the form of a bond that is assessed according to the scale of his intentions. This is done to safeguard the boxers' purses and also the payments due to the officials engaged by him at his tournaments, all of which must hold licences in their various categories. A promoter's licence is issued annually at a cost of £10 and if he does not stage at least two commercial tournaments at any one venue during the year for which he is licenced, he is no longer deemed licenced for that venue.

Six days before the advertised date of his show, a promoter must submit to the Board of Control the names of all boxers and officials he has engaged. He must also disclose the total amount of the purse money he has agreed to pay. He cannot advertise a bout as being for a championship or an eliminating contest for a championship without the sanction of the Board of Control and he is not permitted to stage a title contest until he has promoted at least four tournaments in the previous twelve months, this being a precaution to prevent a fly-by-night promoter from snatching a lucrative championship bout from a more legitimate promoter. In fact, the wise promoter does nothing and takes no step without being in close touch with his controlling body, for his own sake and the good of the sport.

The promoter finds himself beset with very necessary obligations. For instance, he must engage the services of boxers to provide emergency bouts if those advertised end very quickly.

THE PROMOTER

The promoter must have a plentiful supply of gloves at each show, because it is not permitted for a set to be used more than once during any tournament. Also, he must not advertise a foreign boxer as a champion of his country unless he is fully satisfied that he has the right to do so. No more than three alien boxers may appear on any one programme, except where the cost of same is £5,000 or more, when the number engaged can be increased to four.

In the event of a boxer being disqualified, his agreed purse money must be withheld, except for bare travelling expenses, and forwarded to the Area Council of the Board of Control. The boxer is then summoned to appear before his Council when the case is fully discussed. In the event of the boxer being unable to find any excuse for breaking the rules by committing a foul, he can be fined, the amount so conviscated being put into a special fund for the furtherance of the sport or diverted to the Benevolent Fund which helps boxers, past and present, who may need financial aid.

When he comes to assess his personal earnings from a tournament, the promoter must make allowances for the tax he must pay the controlling body, which of course needs a regular income to enable it to function. This tax is scaled according to the takings and when these exceed £2,500, the B.B.B. of C. receives 5 per cent of the money paid to the boxers receiving the largest purses, after the deduction of set expenses, plus 5 per cent of the box-office receipts, after deducting the aforementioned purse money and a graded scale of expenses allowed the promoter. When the takings are under £2,500 and no championship contest is involved, the promoter pays a far lower rate of tax, as little as £4 when up to £500 is taken and only as much as £50 for gate receipts under £2,500. When a promoter pays tax and a boxer receives a purse of £500 or more, the promoter must deduct 5 per cent of the fighter's pay, after allowing training expenses, and forward the residue to the Board of Control. In the event of a promoter sustaining a financial loss on a tournament he is entitled to make a claim for a refund of the whole or part of the tax he has paid to the controlling body. In the event of a promoter failing to promote a tournament, after he has applied for and been granted a specific date, he runs the risk of a penalty.

Promoter/ Boxer Contract

The contract between a promoter and a boxer is a complicated affair and has to be made out on a printed form obtainable from the controlling body. As an example, and as good as any in the world, although there may be slight differences of a minor nature because of national traditions and legislation, the format adopted by the British Boxing Board of Control can be taken as a reliable guide. After agreeing to appear and box on a particular date, either in the afternoon or in the evening, at a specified arena, and over a certain number of rounds (either of two or three minutes duration), and against a named opponent or a suitable substitute, if such is required, the fighter pledges himself to weigh-in at a set weight (usually at one o'clock on the date of the contest) and agrees to make the poundage required, to reduce to that weight within an hour if he is too heavy at the time of scaling, and to pay forfeit to his opponent if he fails, the amount set being stated in the contract. The promoter must also have an identical contract signed by the opposing boxer, who will be liable to pay a forfeit if he is unable to make the stipulated weight. In the case of a boxer being excessively overweight, the Board of Control's representative has the right to take any action deemed necessary, even to the extent of refusing to allow the contest to take place.

There is also a clause whereby should the boxer fail to appear and go through with the fight as arranged, or the contest does not take place because he does not weigh-in correctly, he is liable to pay a specified amount as damages to the promoter or any such additional amount as the controlling body may assess. On the other hand, should the promoter fail to supply a duly qualified opponent, he must indemnify the boxer a sum of money as damages as set out in the contract, plus an additional amount if the Board of Control thinks same is necessary.

A boxer failing to appear at a tournament at the time specified in his contract with the promoter, or otherwise notified by him in writing by the promoter or his matchmaker, is considered to have broken regulations.

Clause 8 is divided into two sections. A – In consideration for boxing as above the promoter shall pay to the boxer the sum of $(£)......... or ...... per cent of the gross receipts if he wins the said contest. $(£)......... or ...... per cent of the gross receipts if he loses, and $(£)......... or ...... per cent of the gross receipts if the said contest is drawn. For the purpose of this agreement the gross receipts do not include any fee payable in respect of radio broadcasting, television or film showing. B – The promoter shall deduct such sum as may be payable to the Board of Control.

When there are ancillary rights appertaining to a contest, such as radio, television or films, each boxer will receive $22\frac{1}{2}$ per cent of the amount forthcoming and 15 per cent will go to the Board of Control which undertakes to set aside one-third of this money in a special fund set up to assist promoters in such manner as the B.B.B. of C. shall decide. Another clause states that on the signing of the contract the boxer must deposit an agreed sum with the Board of Control or his Area Council as a guarantee of his appearance and his compliance with the conditions of the contract. In the event of the contest taking place, the sum deposited is returned to the boxer. The boxer also undertakes not to box publicly an agreed number of days before the date of the contest without the consent in writing of the promoter.

The contract also calls upon the boxer to notify the promoter immediately if by any chance he should find himself unfit to box and therefore unable to carry out his part of the agreement. He must supply a medical certificate. It is his duty to keep in touch with the promoter and to let him know when he is fit to box so that a new date may be arranged. During the time he is unfit the boxer cannot enter into a contract for another contest and, if the cause of his unfitness is due to his own misconduct, he must appear before the Area Council, who will deal with him as it thinks fit. The contract also states the exact time the boxer must put in an appearance at the arena on the day of the contest. Free admission is allowed to his seconds and should he be working on a percentage basis, he is entitled to bring a pre-arranged number of people to look after his financial interests.

In the event of the tournament being staged in the open air and has to be postponed owing to inclement weather or adverse industrial action, the promoter is liable to pay the boxers concerned reasonable expenses they may have incurred in training. It will be appreciated that a promoter takes far greater risks with an outdoor promotion, especially in Britain, although his monetary rewards should be far more because of the larger crowds that can be accommodated. Naturally his organisation has to be increased and perfected for the handling of a large-scale promotion and I have known a promoter to hold a dress rehearsal on a Sunday afternoon prior to staging a mammoth show a day or two later. That it was worth going to this trouble was evidenced when he opened his gates at 6 p.m. and ticket-holders were able to come in at any time up to the start of the main event and walk straight into their allotted seats as simply as if they were going into an indoor arena, while the whole programme went through like clockwork and with no waiting.

One protection that a promoter gets in his contract with a boxer is covered by a clause that gives him an option of booking the fighter for two further contests under the same terms and conditions, both to take place within seven weeks of the original bout. Such arrangements have to be mutually agreed, otherwise the Board of Control is there to sort things out amicably. Again the option clause is there to prevent a rival promoter from 'poaching' a boxer who has risen to the heights and gained immense publicity whilst fighting under the banner of another.

Whilst all the officials at a tournament are appointed by the Board of Control, their fees are paid by the promoter, i.e. the referee, timekeeper, two seconds (one for each corner) and the doctor who passes the boxers medically, both before and after a contest. The announcer, the dressing-room whip and the stewards are engaged by the promoter of his own choice. The promoter usually provides facilities for the press, setting aside a room where they can enjoy his hospitality both before and after a tournament. They must apply to him for ringside accommodation.

Agents for Visiting Boxers

It is essential that any boxer visiting another country for the purpose of participating in a contest, championship or otherwise, should have a registered agent in that country, possessing a current licence issued by his controlling body. This is to ensure that the visiting boxer is fully informed as to the rules and regulations to which he must adhere during his stay, both in and out of the ring, the agent being wholly responsible for their strict enforcement. The agent is also fully responsible for the manager of the visiting boxer, or any other person who accompanies him in an official capacity. The agent must also have available at all times the services of an interpreter if the agent himself is unable to converse in the language of the foreign fighter, or the manager or anyone of responsibility in his party is incapable of conversing in the language of the country being visited.

The agent must acquaint the visiting boxer with all the conditions prevailing for boxing in the country foreign to himself, emphasising any outstanding differences there may exist between the two countries concerned. He must inform the boxer of his obligation regarding the weigh-in for the contest, must make certain that the boxer, his manager, or anyone who may accompany him into his corner, holds an up-to-date licence with the ruling body in his own country and that the boxer holds a current medical certificate declaring that he is physically fit to take part in a boxing contest. The agent must also attend the weighing-in ceremony, be in the dressing-room both before and after the contest, and be at the ringside throughout the whole duration of the contest. He must also ensure that whatever is taken into the corner for the purpose of administering to the boxer in the intervals between the rounds is fully in accord with the regulations laid down by the controlling body of the country being visited. The agent is also held responsible for seeing that the visiting boxer and his officials are properly licensed by the controlling body under whose jurisdiction he is fighting. Agency agreements between an agent and an alien boxer and/or manager must be registered with the controlling body in question.

Mickey Duff (right) knows all there is to know about the Fight Game as he has been engaged in it in one phase or another since his schooldays. He boxed both professionally and successfully as a featherweight in the late 1940's, but he has shown his greatest ability as a world-wide matchmaker since hanging up the gloves. With him is Mike Barrett, one of Britain's leading promoters.

THE PROMOTER
Famous Promoters

(Alphabetical and not prestige order)

Ahlqvist, Eddie. He managed Ingemar Johansson, and became Sweden's leading promoter.

Barrett, Mike. Former dock owner whose love of Boxing induced him to promote at the Manor Place Baths at Walworth. He was so successful with his organisation and match-making that he ventured into big Boxing at the Albert Hall where he stages regular shows, giving every opportunity to promising boys and offering attractive programmes that have reached world championship status.

Best, Johnny. Involved in Merseyside Boxing from youth, taking over the renowned Liverpool Stadium at Pudsey Street in 1929. Three years later he encouraged the building of a more modern arena bearing the same name. It was built on the site of a cemetery, near Exchange Railway Station and, because of the number of sensational upsets there, became known as 'The Graveyard of Champions'. Produced

many great British fighters, including Nel Tarleton, Peter Kane, Dom Volante, Ernie Roderick, etc. Used Anfield Park, Liverpool Football Club's ground, for the staging of major shows, including world championships.

Cochran, Charles B. Renowned theatrical impressario, especially musical shows, became interested in Boxing following World War I and was the

first to offer big purses to prominent boxers. Made the Albert Hall a popular fight arena, his chief interest being in heavyweights. At the Holborn Stadium he presented the famous contest between Georges Carpentier, of France, and Joe Becket, the British champion, charging 25 guineas for a ringside seat, considered a prohibitive price in those days, especially as the bout lasted only 74 seconds. There is a story that one ringsider dropped his programme at the start of the contest and by the time he had picked it up Becket had been knocked out and it was all over without him having seen a blow struck. Cochran staged two world championship matches at Olympia, London, in the first in 1914 Freddie Welsh won the lightweight title from Willie Ritchie, of America, and in the second, 13 years later, Mickey Walker successfully defended his middleweight crown by knocking out Tommy Milligan in the 10th round.

Coffroth, James J. Started as a ringside reporter at the Corbett *v.* Fitzsimmons world heavyweight title bout at Carson City, Nevada, in 1897. Began promoting at San Francisco in a small way, but when the no-decision law was introduced into New York, all the fighting men flocked to California to box under Coffroth's banner. He staged title fights in the Mechanics' Pavilion in San Francisco and in a large outdoor arena at Colma. Because of his luck with good weather he became known as 'Sunny Jim' Coffroth. One of his favourite boxers was Stanley Ketchel, the hard-punching middleweight champion of the world, another was the renowned Battling Nelson, the lightweight kayo king. He was the only man to stage a championship fight over 23 rounds. This came about because Owen Moran, of Birmingham, and Abe Attell, of San Francisco, had fought a draw over 25 rounds. A return fight was called for, but while Moran was prepared for another 25-rounder, Attell wanted the distance reduced to 20. To satisfy both men, Coffroth split the difference to 23 rounds which again ended in a draw.

Dickson, Jeff. Young American, who stayed over from World War I to become leading promoter in Europe. Mississippi-born, the River Showboats must have inspired his colourful match-making. Made his headquarters in Paris where he altered a cycle race track into the *Palais des Sports* to pro-

mote regularly, using fistic stars from all over the universe and staging many world championship battles. Was responsible for introducing Primo Carnera, the giant Italian, to the Boxing scene. Took over the Albert Hall for regular shows and also used the White City Stadium as a boxing arena for the first time, staging such famous fights as Jack Petersen v. Len Harvey, Petersen v. Jack Doyle, Carnera v. Larry Gains. Lost life during service with the U.S. Air Force in World War II.

Elvin, Arthur. Former cigarette kiosk owner at Wembley Exhibition in 1924, he conceived the idea of building a great sports stadium on the site and did so when he opened Wembley Pool & Sports Arena ten years later. Staged two world championships there, John Henry Lewis v. Len Harvey for the light-heavyweight title and Benny Lynch v. Small Montana for the flyweight crown. Also promoted a mammoth show in nearby Wembley Stadium, home of the F.A. Cup, in which Jack Petersen fought a sensational return battle with Walter Neusel, of Germany. Was a great believer in heavyweight novice competitions.

Hulls, Sydney. Came from a Boxing family, his father having been a ringside journalist as well as a wellknown referee. Used the Crystal Palace in South London successfully before taking over the matchmaking at Wembley Arena. Afterwards moved to Harringay Arena where he staged the famous lightweight title fight between Eric Boon and Arthur Danahar. Brought Max Baer, former world

champion to England and gave Tommy Farr the chances to rise to fame and challenge Joe Louis for the world heavyweight title. His greatest promotion was the Len Harvey v. Jock McAvoy match at the White City in July 1939 which was labelled as for the vacant light-heavyweight championship of the world, with attendance estimated at 80,000.

Jacobs, Harry. An East End of London showman who was involved in the transforming of 'Wonderland', an indoor amusement centre in the Whitechapel Road, into a popular Boxing arena that staged twice weekly shows at cheap prices for many years until the place was burned down in 1911. Almost immediately changed a warehouse into a Boxing hall which he named 'Premierland' and continued with his fistic offerings with such success that he was able to obtain a lease on the Albert Hall where he put on stupendous programmes, upwards of a hundred rounds that lasted well past the midnight hour. His was the day of championship fights that were scheduled for twenty rounds

and he produced many outstanding boxers, Phil Scott, Teddy Baldock, Tommy Milligan, Harry Mason, Len Harvey and the like. A real showman of the Barnum quality.

Jacobs, Mike. New York concessionaire and ticket scalper, who became such a powerful block-booking ticket buyer that he was able to break into the big time as a promoter. Took control of world Boxing by the possession of one man, Joe Louis, the celebrated Brown Bomber. Once he had made Louis heavyweight champion of the world, he was able to force his way into Madison Square Garden, New York's famous boxing arena, and there set up the 20th Century Sporting Club which virtually held a monopoly of the world titles. Under his direction Louis set up a record 25 title defences in what the press-men called The Bum of the Month Campaign. Once staged a Carnival of Champions at the New York Polo Grounds in 1937 with three world championships in the bantam, feather and welterweight divisions, with a fourth bout at middleweight between Marcel Thil, of France, and Fred Apostoli, of America, which was a title bout in all but name.

THE PROMOTER

King, Don. Throughout America and in Africa there have always been negro promoters; the first to reach world prominence being Don King, a Black Muslim, who via The Nation of Islam (which replaced the Louisville Syndicate that first sponsored Cassius Clay), was made a vice-president of Video Techniques Incorporated and set about selling the services of Muhammad Ali to the highest bidder. Already the world heavyweight championship had been taken over by T.V. companies, the Frazier v. Foreman fight in 1973 being staged at Kingston, Jamaica, with the backing of the Jamaican government as a tourist investment. Suddenly King took the Foreman v. Ali fight from Top Rank and sold it to President Mobuto of Zaire, who sponsored the bout as part of a huge music festival. The boxers were guaranteed five million dollars each and although there were 62,000 fans and the contest was on closed-circuit television around the world, the Zaire Government is reported to have lost six million dollars.

Levene, Harry. Former manager of a number of notable fighters, in particular, Ted Moore, George West, Larry Gains, Ernie Jarvis and Danny Frush. Turned to promoting on a large scale in opposition to Jack Solomons in 1957, bringing over Willie Toweel, from South Africa, to contest the Empire lightweight title with Dave Charnley, the British champion at the Empress Hall, Earls Court. Afterwards operated at the Albert Hall, then was instru-

mental in re-opening Wembley Arena for professional Boxing. With the help of television he was able to become the leading promoter in Great Britain. Staged world heavyweight championship match between Muhammad Ali and Henry Cooper at the Arsenal Football Ground at Highbury, London in 1966.

McIntosh, Hugh D. A Sydney caterer, he promoted cycling and pedestrian events as a side-line, but switched to Boxing when he saw an opportunity to bring a world heavyweight title fight to Australia. Paid Tommy Burns, the champion, the hitherto unheard sum

of £6,000 to defend his title against coloured Jack Johnson and built a special open-air arena at Rushcutters' Bay for the occasion. Fight took place on Boxing Day 1908 and earned McIntosh a fortune, which he re-invested in Boxing, staging big fights in his own country and in London. Because of his big promotorial ideas he was known as 'Huge Deal McIntosh'. Did his utmost to find a 'White Hope' capable of taking the heavyweight championship from coloured Jack Johnson, whom most of the fistic fraternity detested. When he retired from Boxing McIntosh created an innovation by opening a string of 'Black and White' milk bars throughout London.

Norris, Jim. Madison Square Garden in New York, the centre for world boxing for so many years, had its own boxing promoter from time to time, but frequently leased it to other major promoters, especially those who had control over the heavyweight champion of the day, i.e. Tex Rickard with Jack Dempsey, Mike Jacobs with Joe Louis and Jim Norris with Rocky Marciano. The last-named was a millionaire industrialist, who formed the International Boxing Club and quickly created a monopoly of boxers and contests with the aid of television sponsors. This enabled him to take over major stadiums in many American cities, whilst maintaining a closed shop among champions and their challengers. Finally his power was removed by a Federal judge following an enquiry in 1957 that found Norris and his associates guilty of violating anti-trust laws in monopolising and controlling world championship bouts, fighters and arenas to the detriment of the sport.

Rickard, George (**Tex**). Noted gambler and former Texan rancher, he put the small mining town of Goldfield, Nevada, on the map when he staged a fight for the world's lightweight title between Joe Gans, the holder, and Oscar 'Battling' Nelson in 1906. Everyone thought him mad when he put up 30,000 dollars as purse money and piled it up in a heap of gold coins in his office window. But the receipts were 69,715 dollars and after that he was sold on Boxing, going to New York to outbid all other promoters for the controversial fight between Jeffries and Johnson in 1910 by offering a purse of 101,000 dollars. Took over world boxing and built a huge arena in Jersey

City to stage the first Million Dollar Gate when Jack Dempsey defended his heavyweight title against Georges Carpentier. Takings exceeded two million dollars when he matched Dempsey with Gene Tunney in Chicago in 1927.

Rothenburg, Walter. He put Germany on the boxing map. He was followed by various syndicates with no outstanding personality, in fact, Harry Levene has staged important fights in Germany. Other well-known German promoters are Wilfred Schulz (Hamburg), Willy Knorzer (Hamburg), Gottert & Gretzschel (Berlin).

Solomons, Jack Boxed as a youth, but decided it was far more remunerative to manage boxers and promote fights. Ran a small, but very popular arena in Hackney known as the Devonshire Club with Sunday afternoon shows that produced many outstanding boxers including Eric Boon. Moved into the Big Time after World War II starting with a heavyweight title fight at White Hart Lane, the Tottenham Hotspurs' F.C. ground, between Jack London and Bruce Woodcock. Took the Albert Hall and ran weekly shows there and at the same time promoted more impor-

tant tournaments at the 11,000 seater Harringay Arena. Each year he staged a mammoth show during Derby Week at the White City, his organisation being the acme of perfection. His greatest moment was when Randolph Turpin beat Sugar Ray Robinson for the world middleweight title at the Exhibition Hall, Earl's Court, with a capacity attendance of 18,000. When Harringay was closed to Boxing he moved to Wembley Arena, but subsequently gave up public shows and concentrated on the World Sporting Club, his own creation with headquarters at Grosvenor House in Park Lane. Staged world title bouts at all weights and took Turpin, Freddie Mills, Don Cockell and many others to

world prominence. Promoted shows in aid of the National Playing Fields which the Duke of Edinburgh attended. Invested with the O.B.E. in 1978 for his services to Boxing.

Vienne, Theo. The first major promoter in France in pre 1914 days was Theo Vienne, but usually tournaments and big fights were staged by syndicates. After 1918, Jeff Dickson took over to become the leading promoter in Europe with headquarters in Paris, he also dominated the London scene from 1929–39 at the Albert Hall and White City. After World War II in which he was killed, Gilbert Benaim took over and still remains the leading promoter in France. Rene Levine (Paris) is another well-known French promoter.

Wilson, Arnold. Served apprenticeship as a promoter at the original Liverpool Stadium, then became right-hand man to Charles Cochran, afterwards taking over the Holborn Stadium and the Albert Hall to become London's leading promoter. Had a lot of faith in Joe Beckett and was responsible for his return fight with Georges Carpentier at Olympia which ended disastrously for the British champion in 60 seconds

flat. Also matched Ted (Kid) Lewis with Carpentier in a most lucrative promotion with the main contest ending in round one. Bankrupted himself when he booked the newly-opened Wembley Stadium for a contest between Jack Bloomfield and Tommy Gibbons of America, the attendance being far below the anticipated 110,000. For the first time he had made a match that lacked public appeal as Gibbons was unknown outside his own country although he had just stayed 15 rounds with Jack Dempsey for the world title. Wilson's greatest moments were when he staged the return fight between Beckett and Frank Moran, the Pittsburgh Dentist, one of the fiercest heavyweight battles of all time, and the night little Bugler Harry Lake from Plymouth took the European crown from Charles Ledoux, the tough Frenchman who had been the scourge of British bantams for many years.

THE AUTHORITIES

The Rules of Boxing throughout the world are based on the original rules for glove-fighting first introduced by the Marquess of Queensberry in 1865, revised by the National Sporting Club in 1891, and subsequently amended from time to time by the British Boxing Board of Control to meet the occasion.

There are slight differences prevailing in other countries, but basically they are the same. There are more weight classes nowadays, especially in the Far East where men are on the small side generally and there are other innovations – such as the 'no-foul' rule in America; the standing count in both Europe and America; the three knockdowns in a round that terminates a contest (other than one for a world title in America) in most countries outside Great Britain. There is also the rule that says a referee must continue counting when the bell has sounded to interrupt his count, but which is not practiced much outside Great Britain.

The referee and two judges method of scoring as operates in America, or the three judges and non-voting referee system that operates in Europe and elsewhere.

The principal thing to remember is that if a British boxer is fighting an ordinary contest abroad, he must abide by the local rules. If, however, he is boxing for a European crown, he does so under the European Boxing Union's rules, and if for a world title, the rules as laid down by either the World Boxing Association or the World Boxing Council according to whichever body is controlling the bout. American boxers fighting other than world title contests must do so under the rules of the State Commission in whose territory he is fighting, all of which have slight variations, if only to be different.

On the reverse side, a British boxer fighting for a world or European title in Great Britain, does not box under the B.B.B. of C. Rules, but the generally accepted rules of the E.B.U., W.B.A. or W.B.C. It must be stressed that to avoid confusion, the referee of a title contest always visits a foreign boxer in the dressing-room prior to the start of the contest and instructs him as to any special differences there may be in the rules under which he will be competing.

To show the complete variation in the rules covering every country that permits pro boxing, or the various Unions, Associations and Federations that govern the sport, would occupy far too much space as there are so many, moreover, there would be 90 per cent over-lapping and the services of an interpreter would be necessary. Also, it would never be up-to-date as minor alterations to the rules, mainly domestic, are constantly taking place.

Constant rivalry

Every boxer, manager, promoter, trainer, second, in fact, all those connected in any active capacity in the sport of Boxing, must hold a licence issued by the governing body in his country. Every European nation that permits professional Boxing has its own controlling association and all are affiliated to the European Boxing Union, known prior to 1946 as the International Boxing Union. The World Boxing Council was set up in 1963. At the present time ninety four countries are affiliated to the W.B.C., including the American states of California, Texas and Nevada. The setting up of the W.B.C. was the outcome of the constant rivalry for power in American Boxing which has existed since 1927 when a number of States that objected to the monopoly of the world championships by New York, formed the National Boxing Association.

Ever since there has been times when two world champions at the same weight have been recognised. In 1962 the N.B.A. changed its name to the World Boxing Association to give itself mundane influence, which it asserted in 1965 when deposing

The List of World Champions shown here makes interesting reading and shows the rise of World Champions from the emergent nations such as Mexico and Nicaragua, along with the shift away from the dominance held by the United States of America in 1928 and 1948.

1928

FLYWEIGHT		
Frankie Genaro	USA	NBA
BANTAMWEIGHT		
Charles Bud Taylor	USA	NBA
Bushy Graham	USA	NYBC
FEATHERWEIGHT		
Tony Canzoneri	USA	NBA
Andre Routis	France	NBA
JUNIOR LIGHTWEIGHT		
Ted Morgan	USA	NBA
LIGHTWEIGHT		
Sammy Mandell	USA	NBA

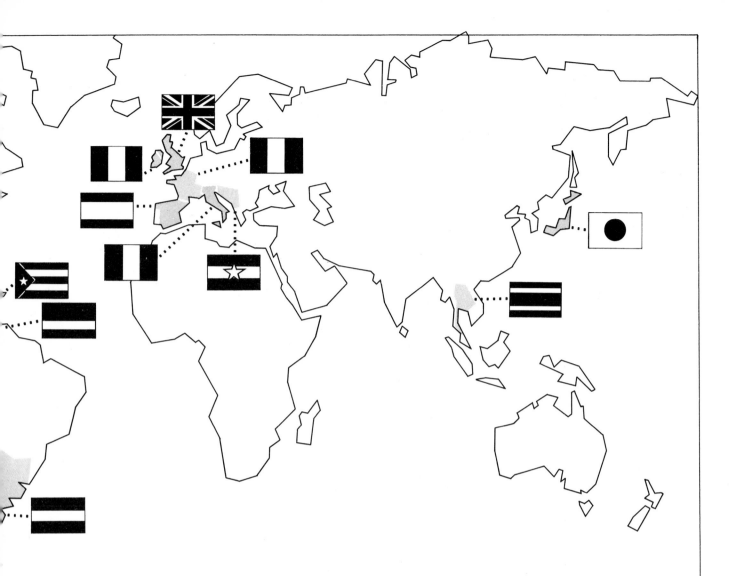

JUNIOR WELTERWEIGHT		
Mushy Callahan	USA	NBA

WELTERWEIGHT		
Joe Dundee	USA	NBA

MIDDLEWEIGHT		
Mickey Walker	USA	NBA

LIGHT HEAVYWEIGHT		
Tommy Loughran	USA	NBA

HEAVYWEIGHT		
Gene Tunney	USA	NBA

1948

FLYWEIGHT	
Rinty Monoghan	Ireland

BANTAMWEIGHT	
Manuel Ortiz	USA

FEATHERWEIGHT	
Willie Pep	USA
Sandy Saddler	USA

LIGHTWEIGHT	
Ike Williams	USA

WELTERWEIGHT	
Sugar Ray Robinson	USA

MIDDLEWEIGHT	
Tony Zale	USA

LIGHT HEAVYWEIGHT	
Gus Lesnevich	USA
Freddie Mills	G.B.

HEAVYWEIGHT	
Joe Louis	USA

1978
(At the time of going to press).

LIGHT FLYWEIGHT		
Freddie Castillo	Mexico	WBC
Yoko Gushiken	Japan	WBA

FLYWEIGHT		
Miqual Canto	Mexico	WBC
Gustavo Espada	Mexico	WBA

BANTAMWEIGHT		
Carlos Zarate	Mexico	WBC
Jorge Lujan	Panama	WBA

SUPER BANTAM		
Wilfredo Gomez	Puerto Rico	WBC
Soo Hwan Hong	Korea	WBA

FEATHERWEIGHT		
Danny Lopez	USA	WBC
Cecilio Lastra	Spain	WBA

JUNIOR LIGHTWEIGHT		
Alexis Arguello	Nicaragua	WBC
Samuel Serrano	Puerto Rico	WBA

LIGHTWEIGHT		
Roberto Duran	Panama	WBC / WBA

LIGHT WELTERWEIGHT		
Saensak Muangsurin	Thailand	WBC
Antonio Cervantes	Colombia	WBA

WELTERWEIGHT		
Carlos Palomino	Mexico/USA *Dual Nationality*	WBC

LIGHT MIDDLEWEIGHT		
Rocky Mattoli	Italy/Australia *Dual Nationality*	WBC
Eddie Gazo	Nicaragua	WBA

MIDDLEWEIGHT		
Rodrigo Valdes	Colombia	WBA / WBC

LIGHT HEAVYWEIGHT		
Mate Parlov	Yugoslavia	WBC
Victor Galindez	Argentina	WBA

HEAVYWEIGHT		
Mohammad Ali	USA	WBC
Leon Spinks	USA	

Muhammad Ali (Cassius Clay) because of his refusal to accept service in the United States Army. Thus, for the first time the heavyweight championship was without a titleholder. The W.B.A. then named Ernie Terrell of Atlantic City, New Jersey, as champion, but he was defeated by Ali, who thus re-established himself as the rightful heavyweight king. In 1967, however, following Ali's indictment by a Federal Grand Jury, both the W.B.A. and the W.B.C. organised eliminating tournaments that resulted in two heavyweight champions being recognised, Jimmy Ellis by the W.B.A. and Joe Frazier in New York. Fortunately this ridiculous state of affairs was ended when Frazier defeated Ellis, but it has gone on in the other divisions so that today most of the weight classes have duel claimants to a world crown, a state of affairs that may never be put right owing to the vast income to be derived from the televising of Boxing, and as a result, when there are two champions at every weight, plus in-between championships that have been created solely to enhance public appeal, the more opportunities there are for staging title fights. The British Boxing Board of Control was at one time affiliated to the National Boxing Association of America. B.B.B. of C. were Founder Members of the World Boxing Council.

The many Boxing Commissions throughout the world are attached to either the W.B.A. or the W.B.C., whichever suits them best, either geographically or because of vested interests or connections. But the majority of the controlling bodies do have working arrangements between themselves, similar to Interpol, so that only boxers licenced in their country of origin can be fistically employed in others. This means that a boxer who forfeits his licence or is under suspension through misdemeanour, accident, old-age, or for his own physical and mental welfare, cannot continue to fight in any other country or state.

British Boxing Board of Control

Prior to the formation of the National Sporting Club in London in 1891, when Boxing in Great Britain was just emerging from the bare-knuckle era, there was no recognised authority to control the sport. Because of its affluent membership however, and autocratic attitude to the fistic profession, the N.S.C. became generally regarded as the Headquarters of British Boxing, in

fact, it was the Mecca for every fighting man and to be engaged to box there was the height of a young boxer's aspirations. As time went on, and with its power diminishing because of the competition aroused by the arrival of commercialised promoters with large arenas and bigger purses to offer, the N.S.C. tried to maintain its grip on the sport by setting up in 1918 a so-called British Boxing Board of Control.

This received no official recognition and was lightly regarded by the boxing fraternity and the press, mainly because the N.S.C.'s domination of the sport was still too much in evidence. In 1929, however, the B.B.B. of C. was reconstituted and gradually assumed complete authority over Boxing in Great Britain, due mainly to its democratic principals, the soundness of its Stewards and the inspiring work of its first general secretary, Charles Donmall, who had a great deal to do with the sketching out of the regulations and dividing the United Kingdom into areas that made its administration easily workable. With variations to meet the changing times, these original regulations remain unaltered.

The Stewards of the British Boxing Board of Control (which includes its President and two Vice-Presidents) have no financial interest in professional Boxing. Their purpose is to control and regulate the sport in Great Britain; to encourage its promotion and to safeguard the interests of its licence holders, both at home and abroad, especially in regard to European and World Championships. They hold regular monthly meetings, plus an Annual General Meeting at which all licence-holders are entitled to attend and Area Councils may submit amendments, additions, or alterations to the existing Rules and Regulations, the acceptance of non-acceptance of which are decided by vote. The Stewards have powers to decide all complaints between licence-holders, to settle disputes and to deal with any misconduct among its members. Although the B.B.B. of C. has no legal standing, it accepts responsibility for all actions and matters that occur within its confines in connection with the promoting of professional boxing contests and tournaments.

Right from its inception, the B.B.B. of C. has instituted a Benevolent Fund that gives financial and other help, principally to ex-boxers, but also to those who have suffered temporary

incapacity, and other licence-holders who may require monetary assistance. There is an Honorary Grants Committee that meets monthly and debates each application on its merits and dispenses such aid as appears necessary to meet each case. I was a member of this Committee for a number of years and eventually became its Chairman and no genuine appeal for help was ever rejected. I am also pleased to record that during this lengthy period it was very gratifying to find the number of applications steadily reducing year by year, a great tribute to the care and attention given to the modern boxer, especially in Great Britain. The money the Benevolent Fund uses comes mainly from disciplinary fines, amateur referees' fees, or from any other source the Stewards may decide.

Apart from the annual fees it receives from licence-holders, the British Boxing Board of Control has other forms of revenue, such as the percentage it takes from boxers' purses and promoters' profits. With this money it has the upkeep of its administrative offices and the general expenses involved in carrying out its objectives. In addition, it supplies championship trophies in the form of the Lonsdale Belts for British titles and cups or other emblems for Commonwealth, European or World championship bouts that take place in Great Britain.

Championship Belts

The practice of awarding Belts as emblematic of championship holding is a long-established tradition that began in the days of the Prize Ring when they were paid for by public subscription or wealthy patrons of the sport. The Belts that denoted a Champion of England were handed down from one titleholder to the next and this practice has been followed ever since throughout the world.

Perhaps the Lonsdale Belts are best known and hold the highest rating in the world of Boxing, even if they are emblematic of only British championships. First introduced by the National Sporting Club in 1909, they were named after the President, Lord Lonsdale, the 5th Earl, who paid for the first out of his own pocket. The holder of one of these trophies must defend same when called upon to do so by the Board of Control, every six months if a challenger is available, or forfeit same. To win one outright he must make two successful defences of his title in bouts recognised officially as championship contests. These need not necessarily be consecutive victories. When he has made a Lonsdale Belt his own property the boxer is entitled to a pension of one pound per week from the age of fifty. The winners of other trophies presented by the B.B.B. of C. become the outright possession of the man to whom they are awarded.

When the Board of Control was reconstituted in 1929, a fresh set of Belts were circulated as and when required. They are made in silver-gilt, i.e. hallmarked standard silver gold-plated and cost at the present time over a thousand pounds. Each carries a portrait of the Earl of Lonsdale at the centre and there are panels on which the winners and dates can be recorded. Each trophy is made up of more than 240 separate pieces, each hand shaped, its assembly being a test of patience as well as skill and craftmanship.

For a long time Eric Boon, the famous Chatteris blacksmith, held the record of winning a B.B.B. of C. Lonsdale Belt outright in the shortest time, i.e. 11 months and 24 days, in 1938-39. But since his day the shortage of active boxers has enabled men to win these trophies a lot quicker, Howard Winstone, the Merthyr stylist, taking only 312 days to win a second Belt outright, although the first occupied 12 months and 28 days. Next quickest to make a Lonsdale trophy his own property was Joey Singleton, from Kirkby in Lancashire, and he engaged in only 16 pro bouts. Several boxers have won two Lonsdale Belts outright, but the only one to win three was Henry Cooper. Ernie Roderick, from Liverpool, was the first boxer to qualify and receive a retirement pension at the age of fifty in 1964.

While many other countries donate belts and trophies to their champions, the only other well-known emblems of authority are the belts issued by the *Ring Magazine* in New York, U.S.A. to all world title-holders irrespective of their nationality. These were started in 1922 when Nat Fleischer first produced this monthly magazine as its proprietor and editor. The 'Ring' Belts are handsome if not highly valuable trophies, with a large central plaque topped by the American Eagle, then the Stars & Stripes, followed by the championship title and the name of the winner. On either side are small ornate medallions and two other larger plaques depicting boxers in action, all of them being linked together with metal chains.

There have been a number of famous Belts in Boxing's history. In America, Richard Kyle Fox, owner and editor of *The Police Gazette*, issued a magnificent one which he proposed should be emblematic of the Heavyweight Championship of the World. When he became champion, however, famous John L. Sullivan refused to accept the trophy preferring to accept one from his townsfolk in Boston, claimed to be of gold and containing 397 diamonds, 250 of which went into his name. It was 48 inches in length, the centre piece was a foot square and carried eight pictorial panels. Its worth in 1887 was eight thousand dollars (£1,600) in those days. Holding it up after its presentation to him, Sullivan exclaimed: "Compared with this, the *Police Gazette* Belt is nothing more than a dog collar". Mr. Fox bided his time, however, and when Sullivan lost the championship to James J. Corbett, the Belt was presented to and accepted by the winner. He took it on a theatrical tour, having it put on display in the various towns in which he performed. In 1893 in Indianapolis it was stolen from a shop window and never seen again.

For the equally famous bare-knuckle contest at Farnborough in Hampshire in 1860, between Tom Sayers, the English champion and John C. Heenan of America, a beautifully engraved silver belt was made for presentation to the winner. As the result after 42 rounds was declared a 'draw', a similar belt was made, so that each of the contestants received one. Sayers took his home to London, but Heenan left his behind when he returned to the United States. It came into the possession of Gilbert C. Elliot, a Vice-President of the original B.B.B. of C. and a prominent member of the National Sporting Club. Today it hangs on a wall in the Board Room of the Board of Control.

A number of boxers have been presented with Belts by their admirers and supporters. Ted (Kid) Lewis, the so-styled, Smashing, Dashing, Slashing Kid from London's East End, twice gained a first notch on a Lonsdale Belt, at feather and middleweight, but never succeeded in winning one outright. His friends therefore produced a Belt very similar in appearance to the Lonsdale trophies which was presented to Lewis at *Premierland* (a popular boxing hall) in 1922 by Max Darewski, a famous theatrical star of the day.

American Boxing Commissions

In the United States of America, where Boxing was a major sporting entertainment for the first half of the 20th century and where almost a monopoly of world championships existed, each State, as already intimated, has its separate Boxing Commission with adherence to the World Boxing Association or the World Boxing Council to suit its own convenience. Most of the major cities possess huge arenas, such as the Chicago Stadium, Boston Garden and Madison Square Garden in New York, while the big baseball parks make ideal venues for outdoor promotions.

As London was the centre spot for Boxing in the United Kingdom, so New York became the focal point in America. At first the sport existed under the Horton Law which permitted contests in New York State without any limit as to the number of rounds to be fought, gave referees the right to render decisions and allowed the posting of forfeits and side-bets. The clubs or promoters who staged tournaments did not pay a licence fee and the sport was not controlled by any authority.

Boxing became such an unruly business, however, that the sport was restricted to club membership only and the Frawley Law was instituted which restricted the number of rounds to ten with no result announced at the finish. This was the long era of the No Decision contests when ringside journalists reported their findings in their columns the following day in what became known as 'Newspaper Verdicts'. On these bets were settled according to the specific journal selected by those who wanted to wager on a result. For publicity purposes, therefore, managers of boxers carefully preserved those reports in which their man was named as the winner, and if the contest took place away from the fighter's hometown, the smart manager would telegraph the favourable result to the local newspaper immediately it was known, so that it could appear in the next editions.

While Boxing was restricted under the Frawley Law, not only in New York, but in other places that followed suit, it enabled promoters in other parts of the United States to come into prominence, particularly in San Francisco, California, where many important championship fights were staged from 1900 to 1917 when the Frawley Law was repealed and the

THE AUTHORITIES

Walker Law came into being, named after New York's famous mayor, Jimmy Walker, who introduced it. This did away with the no-decision bouts in New York State, which had never been satisfactory, because a champion could avoid defending his title for as long as he liked, and contests were permitted up to 15 rounds, with a referee and judges to decide the outcome, all subject to the control of a Boxing Commission. The first licenses were issued in 1920 and the first boxer to receive one was Jack Dempsey, the reigning world heavyweight champion.

Following the example set in Great Britain by the B.B.B. of C., the New York Boxing Commission has made many changes in its regulations for the benefit of its licenced boxers and the better control of the sport. It also introduced certain features which are not countenanced in Great Britain. Here are some of the differences – the finger printing of all boxers, a compulsory 30 days suspension for any boxer who suffers a knockout defeat; the use of eight-ounce gloves in all contests; the eight seconds knockdown count (waived in championship matches); the no-foul rule, by which a boxer cannot claim a foul for a low delivery or any other recognised illegal blow; the use of four ropes in all New York rings, instead of the usual three ropes banded together in the centre of each side; the three knockdowns rule which ends a contest when one boxer has been put on the canvas three times in one round.

In 1962 a rule was adopted in New York that gave a ringside doctor the right to enter the ring during any round to examine an injured boxer and to order the referee to stop the fight if he thought it necessary. This power has never been granted to a doctor in Great Britain, it being considered that

a competent referee knows when a boxer has been badly hurt or injured and will send a man to his corner and then call for a doctor to attend to him if required. There is, however, one regulation in New York that could well be adopted elsewhere and that is the compulsory insurance fee that is taken out on every boxer and deducted from his purse money every time he fights. In case of accidental death the estate receives five thousand dollars.

There have been fatalities in the boxing ring ever since the sport began, but the proportion is very low and has steadily decreased as improved methods for the welfare of the fighting men are introduced. It has sometimes been found following the usual enquiries that the unfortunate victim has himself contributed to his demise by a lack of restraint in such indulgencies as alcohol, drugs, and other things that deprive a man of the perfect physical condition that a sport such as Boxing demands. In some States in America a charge of manslaughter is made against the other boxer concerned, he may even be held in jail pending the result of an inquest. But for a great many years now no such procedure operates in Great Britain, although, as already pointed out the sport has never been legalised. Following a fatality, a coroner is usually satisfied with the evidence provided via the British Boxing Board of Control and a verdict of accidental death is recorded.

Dramas, Scandals & Anecdotes

Prior to the First World War, however, it was a common practice at notable contests for a police inspector, accompanied by a uniformed constable, to visit the dressing-room of each of the principal opponents and warn them that if anything untoward should happen to the man they were engaged to fight, they would be held fully responsible by law and liable for prosecution. On the night that Georges Carpentier, the French champion, met Bombardier Billy Wells, the British heavyweight champion, at the National Sporting Club in 1913, the foreign boxer received such a caution, but at that time his knowledge of English was so limited that he failed to understand what the officer of the law was telling him. A newspaper reporter who was in the room, and who had some schoolboy French to hand, then explained that the inspector had come to wish Carpentier the best of luck and that the whole of the London police force

Right: Sugar Ray Robinson being disqualified in the second round for delivering a punch to the kidneys of his opponent, Gerhard Hecht of Germany.

Far Right: Jersey Joe Walcott twice put Joe Louis down in their title contest at Madison Square Garden, New York and earned Referee Ruby Goldstein's verdict at the finish of their 15-rounder. But the two judges voted for Louis who thus kept his crown. But the Brown Bomber thought he had lost and left the ring before the decision was announced, having to be brought back to hear that he was still champion.

looked forward to his victory. To the astonishment of the inspector, Georges sprang to his feet and kissed him on both cheeks, then went out and defeated Wells in the opening round.

Lawful forbearance

The famous case heard at the Central Criminal Court in London on June 28th, 1901 when the National Sporting Club officials and Jack Roberts, a featherweight from Drury Lane, were accused of feloniously killing and slaying Murray Livingstone (otherwise Billy Smith) did much to bring lawful forebearance on the sport of Boxing. At the outset it was stated that the prosecution was undertaken rather with the view of putting a stop to future competitions of this kind than to get any punishment inflicted on the defendants, and that by their verdict the jury would have to say whether competitions of this character, involving risk to human life, should be continued in the future or not. If the competition carried out under the rules of the Club was unlawful, then undoubtedly the defendants were criminally responsible for the death of Smith.

When the jury returned they were asked if they found that death was caused by a knock-out blow and the Foreman replied: "We do not, but that it was the result of an accident". To the question: "Do you find it was a fight or only a legitimate sparring contest?",

the Foreman replied: "That it was a boxing contest". He was asked if they found the defendants "not guilty" and answered "That is so", whereupon the defendants were discharged. After that the police authorities were only concerned that law and order was preserved at boxing tournaments, the interviewing of prominent boxers in their dressing-rooms prior to a widely publicised contest being purely a matter of ritual.

No man is infallible

As in all sports there are results that do not please everyone and when the event is narrowed down to two competitors, the outcome is subjected to the utmost intensity and feeling among the onlookers can run extremely high if it appears that the referee or the judges have erred in their judgment. No man is infallible and boxing referees are no exception with the result that there have been cases when a referee has been disciplined following the rendering of a decision that has caused dissatisfaction among both the spectators and the ruling officials.

There have been and always will be controversial verdicts, but there is one vital point to bear in mind – the fact that the referee in the ring is in the best possible position to judge the merits of the boxers engaged and also to determine which of the pair has had the advantage of any particular round, or if

their successes have been equal. This is the reasoning behind the British Boxing Board of Control's steadfast adherence to the system that gives a referee the sole right to render a verdict at the end of a contest.

Even so, and although it is a regulation that the Referee's decision is final, the B.B.B. of C. has, on occasions, thought fit to use its disciplinary powers over a disputed verdict. There was the 20 rounds contest between Len Harvey, from Plymouth, and Johnny Sullivan, of Covent Garden, which took place at *The Ring* at Blackfriars in South London in 1926 when everyone in the packed arena thought Harvey had gained a clear-cut points decision except Referee Joe Palmer. He was summoned to appear before the Stewards, who cancelled his licence. Referee Arthur Myers, from Manchester, was officially criticised for his handling of the British heavyweight title contest between Jack Petersen, the holder, and Jock McAvoy, the middleweight champion from Manchester, which took place at the Empress Hall at Earl's Court in London in 1936. There have been other incidents of a similar nature but in no instance has a verdict, once rendered, been reversed, except on one occasion when a referee, on leaving the ring, realised that he had made an error in naming the winner and immediately returned to put the matter right to the full approval of the fans.

In other countries, however, a referee's decision has been changed by the boxing authorities on a number of occasions. In Berlin in 1951 the referee disqualified Sugar Ray Robinson for hitting his opponent, Gerhard Hecht, in the kidneys. This brought forth a ringside riot, whereupon the Boxing Commission held an enquiry and twelve hours later the result was announced as 'no contest'. In Columbus, Georgia, U.S.A. in 1923, Referee Harry Ertle declared that Mike McTigue, the reigning light-heavyweight champion of the World had fought a draw with Young Stribling, the local hero. The crowd was so hostile to this decision that the referee changed his mind (under pressure) and announced Stribling as the winner and new champion. As soon as he got out of Georgia, however, the referee again changed the verdict – back to his original declaration of a 'draw'. In Paris in 1911, after a referee had decided that Willie Lewis, an American welterweight, had outpointed the Dixie

THE AUTHORITIES

Left: George Carpentier v. Gunboat Ed. Smith of America in a contest advertised as for the White Heavyweight Championship of the world, Carpentier was put down in the 6th round. Immediately the Frenchman's manager, Francois Descamps, entered the ring claiming a foul.

Below left: Carpentier dropped the Australian champion George Cook for a count at London's Albert Hall. As Cook was dropping the Frenchman drove in another right. Referee Jack Smith counted out Cook giving Carpentier the win by a knockout.

Kid (Aaron Brown) over 20 rounds, a jury of sportsmen who disagreed with the verdict, were successful in having it reversed.

Twice in New York a boxer has taken court action against a decision rendered in favour of his opponent. In 1921, bantamweight Packey O'Gatty was declared to have won on a foul over Roy Moore, but the next day Deputy Commissioner Walter Hook changed the decision to 'no contest' and held up O'Gatty's purse. The boxer took legal action against the Boxing Commission and won his case, the judge deciding that a referee's verdict was final.

In 1952 Referee Ray Miller's score card read that Joey Giardello had won over Billy Graham over ten rounds at Madison Square Garden. Judge Charles Shortell voted for Graham while Judge Joe Agnello scored it as a win for Giardello. Commissioners Bob Christenberry and C. B. Powell at the ringside, then altered Agnello's card, changing it to make Graham the winner and it was duly announced that Billy had won. Giardello then instituted proceedings before the State Supreme Court, whereupon Justice Bernard

Botein ruled that the controlling body had no right to change the scorecard of an official judge, and Giardello was accordingly proclaimed as the winner.

A famous case in which a referee was over-ruled by the two judges occurred when Joe Louis defended his world heavyweight title against Jersey Joe Walcott at Madison Square Garden, New York, in 1947. Ruby Goldstein, a former highly-ranked boxer and respected referee, gave Walcott 7 rounds, Louis 6 with two even. He also scored 15 points for Walcott and 11 for the champion. In Great Britain this would have given Walcott the title, but Judge Monroe's card showed: Rounds, Louis 9, Walcott 6; points Louis 11, Walcott 10. Judge Forbes made it: Rounds, Louis 8, Walcott 6, with one even; points, Louis 9, Walcott 12. Out of these differences Louis was declared the winner on a split decision, but he was so sure he had lost that he was about to leave the ring and had to be brought back to hear himself announced as the winner, whereupon he went over to the unfortunate Walcott and said: "Sorry, Joe". As a point of interest Walcott eventually became

champion four years later, after he had tried five times to win the title.

Controversial incidents
Some boxers get into the controversial limelight more than others. Georges Carpentier was a notable example. In his bout with Gunboat Smith, of America, at Olympia, London, in 1914, he was put down for a count and then received a light cuff on the head – an intended blow which Smith tried hard to pull back. At once, Francois Descamps, the Frenchman's manager, jumped into the ring, claiming that a foul had been committed and Referee Eugene Corri named Carpentier as the winner, a decision that caused a good deal of disagreement. Eight years later at the Albert Hall, there was a similar incident, in reverse. Carpentier knocked down George Cook, the Australian champion, in round four and as the Australian was sinking to the canvas, the Frenchman struck him again on the jaw, knocking him unconscious. There were demands for Carpentier's disqualification, but Referee Jack Smith decided that Georges' punch had struck his rival's jaw before Cook's knees touched the canvas, and so declared the Frenchman the winner by a knockout. The film showing of the contest made it appear that the referee could have been wrong in his judgment, but the result was allowed to stand, in spite of strong protestations from the Australian's supporters.

Just four months after that, the Frenchman was involved in yet another controversial incident. He was defending his world light-heavyweight title against Ted (Kid) Lewis, again at the Albert Hall, and during the first round there was so much holding on both sides that Referee Joe Palmer stopped the contest and for some reason addressed a reprimand to the Englishman. The 'Kid' was so aghast at being considered the culprit, he forgot the first law of Boxing and turned to the

Third Man in abject denial. In doing so he gave Carpentier an excellent look at his chin of which Georges took the fullest advantage, banging over a straight right that knocked Lewis cold. Everyone considered that the Frenchman had earned disqualification, as technically the bout had been stopped while the referee spoke to Lewis, but in spite of howls of disapproval from the fans, who did not like his unsporting gesture, Carpentier got away with it again and was returned as the winner.

The bad boy of sport

There have always been, and will continue to be suggestions that all is not always straight-forward and trustworthy in professional sport and, of course, where the human element is concerned there is always the possibility of a result that breeds suspicion as to its genuine nature. Over the years Horse Racing, Football, Wrestling and Athletics have had their black moments, while Baseball in America has been in doubt on a number of occasions. Even Cricket has not been immune, while the modern Tennis 'circuses' lend themselves to criticism. The Bad Boy of Sport, however, has always been Boxing, probably because only two competitors are involved in any one contest, little thought being given to the fact that behind them may be unscrupulous promoters, managers, seconds and patrons who, like George IV when Price of Wales, liked backing pugilists and did so with vast sums, but had no time for losers.

On numerous occasions during my more than fifty years in close connection with Boxing, I have been told that such and such a fight was 'crooked', that a certain boxer has 'laid down' or that a certain referee has been bribed into giving an incorrect result. There have been enquiries in all parts of the world into events and decisions that have aroused suspicion, particularly in the United States where there have been judicial investigations into Boxing and where it has been proved that criminal influences have been at work. But I could never go into a witness box and swear that to my knowledge any pre-conceived plot to defraud the public has ever occurred in British Boxing. I have known imported boxers to be heavily fined by the Board of Control for allegedly 'not trying' and there have been similar instances where action has been taken by the authorities to protect the fight fan. Eric Boon told me

that he had been approached to 'throw a fight', but had declined to do so, even at the risk of incurring physical injury, whereas Jake LaMotta, world middleweight champion, confessed that he had been paid to lose to Billy Fox in 1947. Al (Bummy) Davis had his dressing-room invaded one day by gangsters calling themselves 'Murder Incorporated', but defied their threats to be dishonest in the ring, the fact that he was murdered by gunmen while endeavouring to protect a cafe owner in a hold-up being purely coincidental. In 1900 Joe Gans, beloved by all in the Fight Game and styled 'The Old Master', was once accused of 'laying down' to 'Terrible' Terry McGovern in two rounds and was ostrasized in Chicago for the rest of his boxing life of more than eight years, but no one could ever prove that he was guilty.

On the whole there is far too much at stake for a boxer to lend himself to duplicity. A defeat, whether genuine or not, is a blot on a record that can never be expunged and no fighting man could bring off a faked contest more than once. Clean records unblemished by losses are the passports to fame and the big money that goes with it. Also, it must be remembered that the average career of a boxer is a small proportion of his entire life, therefore, it is up to him to make the utmost use of it and take no risks that would curtail or injure his earning capacities.

I agree that there have been a number of scandalous happenings in Boxing, but all these took place in the so-called 'good old days' when fighting men were regarded as little more than performing animals by those who put up the money for their services. Looking into the record books we find it hard to believe that men were encouraged to fight so frequently and in so many bouts, Harry Greb, middleweight champion of the world and known as The Human Windmill, engaged in 290 contests and died following an eye operation at the age of 32. On the other hand Johnny Dundee, one-time featherweight champion, engaged in 321 bouts and lived for 72 years. Archie Moore had 228 contests and is still alive at the age of 64. Young Bill Stribling took part in 286 contests and was still an active boxer when killed in a motor-cycle accident at the age of 29. All these instances involved American boxers, but Ted (Kid) Lewis's record shows 253 bouts and he lived to 70, while his long-term enemy, Jack

Britton, had 325 contests and died at the age of 77.

One incident that caused the B.B.B. of C. grave concern was the contest for the British lightweight title between the holder, Billy Thompson, from Hickleton Main in Yorkshire, and Tommy McGovern, from Bermondsey. The pair, who were under the same management, had met 13 months earlier at Hanley when Thompson kept his title by a points decision. This time they met at Wandsworth Greyhound Stadium and it was all over in 45 seconds with McGovern the winner by a knockout. Afterwards the defeated Thompson admitted that he had spent the previous night in a Turkish Bath in an effort to make the stipulated weight of 9st 9lbs (135 pounds). He managed it by a bare four ounces, but the effort had reduced his resistance to such an extent that he was put down from virtually the first punch landed by the winner. Quite obviously anyone in the know about Thompson's weight problem could have made a killing by betting on McGovern.

Sacrificial giant

An American scandal was the way Primo Carnera, the giant Italian, was exploited and robbed during his way to the heavyweight championship. After being launched in Europe he went to New York where he gained two more managers, in addition to the man who had discovered him, and was then taken on a two years tour of the States, in which he engaged in 36 bouts, winning all but five in a few rounds apiece. Twenty-seven bouts in Europe and America followed in the next year, of which he lost only two on points and he was then matched with Jack Sharkey, the reigning champion, at Long Island in 1933. In spite of his long run of so-called successes, the few bouts that had gone any distance were not sufficient to give him the experience to win the championship, yet he did so with a recorded knockout in six rounds. The result was surprising as Sharkey had outpointed Carnera quite convincingly twenty months earlier. But that is not the point of this disclosure.

Primo then went on to defend his title against Paolino Uzcudun in Rome, which should have proved a lucrative engagement, then against Tommy Loughran in Miami, which could not have been for peanuts. Finally he lost his crown to the heavy-punching Max Baer in an open-air attraction at Long

THE AUTHORITIES

Island for which his publicised earnings were 152,146 dollars and 22 cents, which included 17,000 dollars from the radio and film rights. He was then sacrificed to Joe Louis, a man eight years his junior, who picked up 60,433 dollars for stopping Primo in six rounds before 60,000 fans in the Yankee Stadium, one of New York's vast baseball parks. What Carnera got was not published, for the simple reason that by the time he had paid his managers, met his enormous 'expenses' and settled with numerous other hangers-on, he probably finished up in debt. When his boxing career ended a year later he was broke despite his long winning record and four championship fights. He had to turn to so-called and highly pre-arranged wrestling to earn a living and finally ended up running a liquor store in Los Angeles.

Fight to the finish

One notorious scandal that brought about the downfall of the instigators was the heavyweight match between Jem Smith, who claimed to be Champion of England, and Frank Slavin, an Australian. It was sponsored by the Pelican Club of London and advertised as for the Championship of England, with each side putting up £500 (2,500 dollars) the fight to be to a finish with bare knuckles. As prize fights were illegal in England at that time, the contest was staged at Bruges in Belgium, Smith being heavily backed to win by the wealthy Squire Abingdon Baird, who delighted in wagering on fighters and went to every extreme to ensure that they won. Whilst Slavin had a few friends with him, Smith had the support of Baird's disreputable associates, plus a specially hired gang of Birmingham racecourse ruffians.

To win against these odds was asking a lot, but Slavin was made of stern stuff and from the outset had the better of matters. When it seemed almost certain that he would defeat Smith, however, the mob took a hand. Every time Slavin came near the ropes he was struck by sticks and punched with knuckle-dusters, while attempts were made to trip him up. Still the Australian fought on determindly and in the 14th round, when the Englishman was on the verge of being knocked out, the ring was invaded, the unruly mob preventing Slavin from striking another blow. Referee Joe Vesey, who had closed his eyes and ears to seeing that fair play was conducted, thereupon

declared the bout drawn, thus saving the Squire's wager. British sportsmen, in general, however, were so incensed at the foul manner in which Slavin had been treated that they ordered the stake-money to be handed to Frank, and after expelling the Squire from the Pelican Club, withdrew their support thus bringing about its extinction.

Rags to riches

There have been many Rags to Riches stories in the annals of Boxing, mostly in the first half of the century. But many of the men who came from nothing, ended in the same situation, in spite of substantial earnings. There were always too many 'deductions' and what was left they frittered away, being totally unsuited to appreciate the value of money and being lured into financial ventures that no business man would have given a second look at. Boxers in the main are easy prey for the person who is out to relieve them of their hard-won earnings.

A newspaper once printed a story about Joe Louis and Sugar Ray Robinson falling for a scheme to pipeline into New York mineral water from the Rocky Mountains; Randolph Turpin was persuaded to invest in a Welsh hotel and finished up working on a scrap heap owned by the man who had previously employed him; Freddie Mills found himself involved in a Chinese Restaurant; Rocky Graziano, who must have earned a million dollars, was glad to become a television star at the end of his career, while Freddie Welsh, who reigned as world lightweight champion for three years in which he took part in 49 bouts, including two title defences, lost all his earnings in a Health Farm project and died penniless.

These are but a very few instances of boxers being parted from their money, but on the other side of the coin there are outstanding examples of men who have kept the bulk of their purses, such as Gene Tunney, who, before the television era, held the record for collecting 990,000 dollars for a single contest, then retired undefeated for his championship and married an heiress, undoubtedly an object lesson to all fighters! Ill-fated Rocky Marciano was another who had stashed away a considerable fortune before he, too, retired undefeated for the title and in his 49 paid bouts. Henry Cooper kept a tight rein on his earnings following his highly successful career, which included a

world title fight and being Heavyweight Champion of Great Britain, the British Commonwealth and of Europe.

Of course, the biggest ring earner of all-time has been Muhammad Ali, twice heavyweight champion of the world, who came into an era when he could command millions of dollars every time he fought after winning the championship. The boxers since 1945 have had better opportunities to do well financially out of Boxing, but prior to that a man was fortunate who came out of the ring with enough to keep him comfortable for the rest of his life and I recall that little Jimmy Wilde, who did retire with a considerable sum, lost a lot of it by investing with James White, the financier, who eventually went bankrupt.

The Sporting Clubs

Nowadays, particularly in Great Britain, a good proportion of Boxing shows take part in private clubs, most of the small arenas having disappeared, due mainly to the ever-increasing lack of fighting men, plus the monopoly enforced upon those who continue to stage tournaments open to the public. In London, for example, there are three of major importance: the re-established National Sporting Club, with headquarters at the Cafe Royal in Regent Street; the World Sporting Club, which operates at Grosvenor House in Park Lane; and the Anglo-American Sporting Club at the Hilton Hotel a little further south. In most of the provincial cities there are clubs of a similar pattern, the members paying an annual subscription that entitles them to a specified number of tournaments, plus the opportunity to purchase tickets for guests and the luxury of dining before the show starts. Some boxers never appear anywhere but at these closed-door venues that cannot provide the atmosphere and encouragement that prompted boxers to give of their best, and more, in the past.

The most famous boxing club of all time was the original National Sporting Club which opened its doors at the King's Theatre in Covent Garden in 1891 and proved a powerful influence on the sport until it went into liquidation in 1931, forty years of autocratic rule at a time when most needed. The N.S.C. rose from the dying embers of what had become the infamous Pelican Club. It was the brain child of Arthur Bettinson, a former amateur champion, and John Fleming, who had been

Left: Primo Carnera's comeback came to an abrupt end when he was stopped in three rounds by coloured Leroy Haynes on March 16th 1936 and in a return bout was sadly mauled by the same boxer, finally being carried out of the ring in nine rounds at Ebbets Field, Brooklyn, New York.

Below left: At the age of 38 and after being retired for six years Jim Driscoll, former featherweight champion of Great Britain was persuaded to make a comeback against Charles Ledoux, French champion of Europe. Ledoux was eleven years younger, yet Driscoll gave him a boxing lesson for sixteen rounds when his seconds threw in the towel.

associated with the Pelican in its heyday. They set out to control Boxing in Great Britain and make a respectable profession of it, raising it from the disreputable business it had become during the latter days of the Prize Ring. They adopted the Marquess of Queensberry Rules, modified them to meet existing conditions as time went on, established the weight divisions, monopolised the championships and, of course, introduced the famous Lord Lonsdale Belts.

The success of the N.S.C. inspired the formation of similar clubs both in Paris and New York, but they did not last long. Boxing clubs have existed in America since the earliest days of the sport there, but all of them have been commercial ventures run by financially-interested promoting bodies, relying on ticket sales to the general public to keep going. Mike Jacobs started the 20th Century Sporting Club, but the only members were those who had invested money in the venture, and the tournaments staged at Madison Square Garden and in New York's big open-air arenas were all dependent on box-office receipts paid by the fans.

One other famous concern on these lines was the Olympic Club at New Orleans in Louisiana, U.S.A., notable for staging the first heavyweight championship contest under Marquess of Queensbury Rules, i.e. with gloves, in 1892 between John L. Sullivan and 'Gentleman' Jim Corbett. The year previous it had put up the largest purse to date for a contest for the middleweight championship of the world between the holder, Jack Dempsey (The Nonpareil) and Bob Fitzsimmons, which the Cornishman won in 13 rounds and received 1,000 dollars.

Many famous contests took place at the original N.S.C., perhaps the most sensational being the bout between Peter Jackson and Frank Slavin for the British Empire heavyweight title in 1892, which ended in a victory for the former in round ten, and the classic encounter in 1919 between 'Peerless' Jim Driscoll (aged 38) and Charles Ledoux, of France (aged 27) which ended in the famous Welshman's retirement in round 16 from exhaustion, after having won every round up to that point. It was a glorious performance that resulted in the members getting up a testimonial for Driscoll's benefit that reached £4,000 (20,000 dollars).

There has never been, however, a Club to compare with the N.S.C. although its present day counterpart maintains most of its original traditions which include complete silence by the onlookers during the course of a round, a rule that might be considered completely out-of-date and which cannot be commended for providing either the spectacle or the colour which, after all, is what the Fight Game is all about.

THE MEDIA

Like all sports, Boxing relies on the press for its publicity and editors are always prepared to give maximum space to a forthcoming 'Big Fight' or its result, especially if there has been a sensational ending. Until the turn of the century newspapers were the sole medium for conveying reports of contests, although moving-pictures of important bouts had just come into being. These increased in number and quality and, eventually in colour, meanwhile radio allowed the ringside commentary of major fights and then came television to thrill millions of watchers all over the world and cause the earnings of boxers to reach astronomical dimensions.

In spite of the march of time, however, the printed word has always been used to debate the current situation, to discuss matches and to render reports of the exchanges and to pass verdict on the outcome. Back in the days of the Prize Ring, before the advent of the daily newspapers, the news of prominent boxers and the result and description of their contests were conveyed all over England by means of broad-sheets, very often in doggerel rhyme, with crude drawings showing a major feature of the event. These were carried on foot or by horse to the market places and fairs and sold to the followers of The Fancy for a copper or two, the results of some contests being received sometimes months later, but bought as eagerly as were those crude publications describing national events, the affairs of royalty, land and sea battles, that were readily offered by the travelling salesman.

It has already been noted that an account of a Prize Fight was published as early as 1683, but it is difficult to pinpoint a date when the activities of the ring first appeared in the popular press. It does seem, however, that by the time James Fig had reached the height of his fame, his exploits were being featured in the newspapers of the day.

The first of these, *The Daily Courant*, was published in 1702; *The Tatler*, three times weekly, started in 1709, *The Spectator* in 1711 and *The Guardian* began in 1713. All these carried fistic items, especially as the Champion of England was patronised by the Earl of Peterborough and Fig's academy in London was visited by royalty on a number of occasions. Most historians declare that the first book on Boxing was published in 1747 – *A Treatise upon the useful Science of Defence* by Captain Godfrey, who dedicated his work to the Duke of Cumberland, the unsporting backer of John Broughton. In this the gallant Captain wrote: "I have purchased my knowledge with many a broken head and bruises in every part of me", adding: "I chose mostly to go to Fig and exercise with him, partly because I knew him to be the ablest master." This shows that there were others in the business of teaching the Noble Art, therefore there must have been plenty of participants.

In 1894 appeared *The Morning Advertiser*, published by the Society of Licensed Victuallers, a trade that has always supported and given freely of its space to Boxing. Other early newspapers that kept its readers up-to-date with the affairs of the Prize Ring were *The Morning Post* started in 1772 and *The Morning Herald* which began in 1780, while the celebrated Boxing historian, Pierce Egan, claimed that "the most fashionable daily newspaper of the day (probably *The Times* which had its first issue in 1785) enjoyed a happy increase in sales in respect of its containing the genuine correspondence between Humphreys and Mendoza", who had their first encounter in 1788.

Our first full picture of the Prize Ring we owe to the aforesaid Egan, a printer's compositor and later freelance sports reporter, who turned Boxing historian and in 1818 produced *Boxiana* in several volumes subtitled '*Sketches of Antient and Modern Pugilism*', which covered the principal activities of the sport from the days of Fig, a hundred years of bare-fist fighting written in colourful style with full use of the slang of his times. The basis of the material Egan gained from an earlier publication under the same heading which had been printed and published by his employer, George Smeeton, at St. Martin's Lane, London, in 1812.

The Irishman gained further information from Captain Godfrey's 'Treatise' and contemporary broadsheets, newspapers and magazines of the day, also from *Pancratia – A History of Pugilism* by J. B., again produced by Smeeton. From *Blackwood's Magazine* in 1820 we get an estimate of Egan's prestige at that time: "It is sufficient justification of Pugilism to say Mr. Egan is its historian . . . his style is perfectly his own, and likely to remain so, for it is as inimitable as it is excellent. The man who has not read *Boxiana* is ignorant of the power of the English language.

Other famous volumes concerning the events and personalities of the Prize Ring were *Pugilistica* by Henry Downes Miles, published in three volumes in 1880, each containing 500 pages and many illustrations. It enjoyed several editions, the last of which was in 1906. Mr. Miles, who among other literary ventures, was also editor of the *Sportsman's Magazine*, despised Pierce Egan and accused him of slap-dash journalism, and it can be accepted that *Pugilistica* is the more authentic and detailed publication of the two.

The editor of *Bell's Life* in London was another responsible for the activities of the Prize Ring. He brought out *Fights for the Championship* in a single volume, also *Fistiana or The Oracle of the Ring*, a pocket-sized book that contained a list of Prize Fights in chronological order, plus the Rules and the duties of referees, umpire and seconds. It went into several editions, the last of which was in 1864. Another history of bare-fist fighting, produced

THE MEDIA

in two volumes in 1910, was *Fights for the Championship. The Men and Their Times* by Fred Henning, editor of the *Licensed Victualler's Gazette*, which had published the material serially in its pages. Henning was also the author of such works as: *Recollections of the Prize Ring, Trips to Our Training Quarters, Hosts and their Hostelries, Taverns and their Tenants*, etc.

Just as the growing popularity of Boxing was soon recognised by the newspapers, so it is also noteworthy that the theatres saw and recognised its importance as a form of public entertainment, for, as Egan states: "Have not our classic theatres invited Pugilism to their boards and the names of some of the first-rate boxers enriched their play-bills." In 1824 he began publishing *Egan's Life in London & Sporting Guide*, but this was taken over by a certain John Bell, a printer, who had created *Bell's Weekly Messenger*, of which he was both editor and publisher. With the amalgamation of Egan's periodical he brought out *Bell's Life in London* which was the outstanding sporting newspaper in England, devoting the bulk of its space to Horse Racing and Boxing.

It ran until 1886 when it was incorporated in *The Sporting Life*, the great rival to which for many years was *The Sportsman*. Individual newspapers that sprang up at the start of the 19th century could not afford to leave out pugilistic news and I have in my possession copies of *The Alfred* dated 1811 (which presumably was started a year earlier), priced at 6½d and printed and published by W. M. Willett at No. 47 Ludgate Hill, London, one of which contains an eye-witness account of the famous contest between Cribb and Molyneaux. Another popular publication was the *Sporting Telegraph* that began life in 1822.

When Tom Sayers fought John Camel Heenan at Farnborough in 1860 practically every newspaper in England and America printed news stories before the event and whole editions afterwards. All the sporting newspapers carried letters from one prominent pugilist to another in which challenges to fight were made and accepted. Advertisements appeared of a like nature, plus offers by 'professors' to teach the Noble Art, and where and when boxing tournaments could be witnessed at one or another of the many London taverns that had a parlour set aside for displays of fisticuffs, one in particular being the notorious 'Blue Anchor' in Church Street, Shoreditch.

Richard Kyle Fox, of New York, an equal admirer of stage, racecourse and boxing arena, of whom I have already made mention in connection with Boxing Belts, appears to have started his famous *Police Gazette* around 1873. He called it The Leading Illustrated Sporting Journal in America, and all its pictures were artist-drawn and very vivid they were too. It contained sixteen pink pages, size 17½in by 11½, was a weekly and sold for ten cents a copy. In conjunction with it he published his *Police Gazette Sporting Annuals*, containing boxers' records, first as paper-backs, 7¼in by 5in, then as pocket books, 4½in by 3in. They ran up to World War I, together with a number of other cheaply-produced books dealing with the lives of fistic champions and other sporting celebrities, plus a number of harmless but considered *risqué* works devoted to the bright, if seamy side of life.

The Police Gazette enjoyed a large circulation and when British-born Bob Fitzsimmons was about to fight for the Heavyweight Championship of the World, the astute Mr. Fox embarked on a British edition that had its editorial offices in Fleet Street, the first issue coming out on October 3rd 1896, just four months before the great fight,

How the 'Big Fight' is brought to your TV screen

its future being assured when the Cornishman won the title in the 14th round.

The success of the London version of the *Police Gazette* prompted the launching of a weekly paper on very similar lines which the publishers named *The Mirror of Life*. Its first issue appeared on January 1st, 1900 and consisted of 16 uncut pages which could be used as a double-sided table cloth if everyone in the family was sportingly inclined. It, too, favoured the major sports, plus the personalities of the music-hall and theatre. It's editor over a great many years, who later became its proprietor, was Frank Bradley, an amateur boxer of great ability, who was an ardent fight enthusiast and had seen many great contests in America in his youth. When he died in 1923 the paper folded up, (because without him it just could not exist) having met strong competition in a weekly entirely devoted to the Noble Art and aptly but simply known as *Boxing*.

The Berry Brothers were the proprietors of a long-established periodical called *Health & Strength* and the man who contributed boxing items to its pages, John Murray, persuaded them that Boxing could be written up in such a manner that would appeal to the ever-growing public interest in glove fighting. They launched the new paper in September, 1909 and, apart from hazardous periods during two world wars, survives to this day, but under the title of *Boxing News*. It has been my pleasure to twice be its editor and in 1944 the present *Boxing News Annual & Record Book* came into being under my direction.

There had been record books published by the *Sporting Life* in 1910 and 1921 and by *Boxing* in 1914 and 1921, but in nothing like the comprehensive and accurate way in which the *Boxing News* publication is compiled. Jack Solomons, the post-war promoter of such magnitude, gave his name to a very well produced Record Book, the work of L. N. (Bill) Bailey, boxing correspondent to *The Star*. It ran from 1948 to 1953 when it became too expensive to produce. One other annual publication devoted to boxers' records worth noting was the French publication, the *Annuaire Du Ring*, edited by Victor Breyer, journalist and referee, which was started in 1909 and came out each year until 1939. After the Second World War a weekly paper entitled *La Boxe* came into being and this re-issued the *Annuaire Du Ring*

which ran until 1959 when its parent paper ceased publication. France was the first European country to take up Boxing and has always had its magazines and papers devoted to the sport, *l'Echo des Sports* being one of the most popular. Other Continental countries have come forth with Boxing publications from time to time, the most ambitious at the moment being *Pugilato* a handsome and jam-packed annual of more than 600 pages, produced by Giuseppe Ballarati in Rome.

Reverting to America, in 1903 a rival to the *Police Gazette Annual* appeared under the editorship of T. S. Andrews, who came from Milwaukee in the State of Winconsin and styled himself 'America's Greatest Boxing Authority'. This was another pocket-sized production, $5\frac{1}{4}$in by 3in that contained records of all sports although more than half was devoted to Boxing. This petered out in 1937 because of the strong competition it had received from an annual introduced in 1922 by the Everlast Sports Equipment Company of New York. This continued publication until 1937, the same year in which *The Post Record Book*, a rival, ceased publication after seven years.

While the *Police Gazette* was still being published, even after the death of its

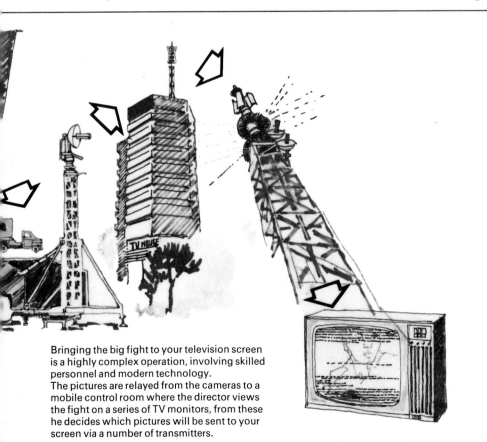

Bringing the big fight to your television screen is a highly complex operation, involving skilled personnel and modern technology.
The pictures are relayed from the cameras to a mobile control room where the director views the fight on a series of TV monitors, from these he decides which pictures will be sent to your screen via a number of transmitters.

Personnel and Equipment used to bring the fight to your screen.

Personnel
Outside Broadcast Director
Lighting Cameraman/Director
5 Cameramen (1 reserve)
5 Soundmen
Commentator
2 Floor Managers
Production Assistant
Slow Motion Operator
2 Links Engineers
4 Engineers
4 Electricians
5 Riggers/Drivers

Cameras
3 Static
1 Handheld

Vehicles
Mobile Control Room
Links Vehicle
Slow Motion Vehicle
Tender

THE MEDIA

founder, a young New York sports writer named Nat Fleischer, an ardent Boxing enthusiast conceived the idea of a monthly, illustrated magazine which he aptly named *The Ring*. This was first published in February, 1922 and has continued without a break ever since. In 1942 he issued his *Ring Record Book and Boxing Encyclopedia*, which covers the sport in its entirety, containing the complete records of every world champion and near champion, plus the modern boxers and a mass of ring data that is brought up-to-date with each issue. Fleischer, who died in 1972, aged 84, gave more to Boxing than any man before him since Pierce Egan. He founded the Hall of Fame and over his long association with the sport collected together his famous Museum which is visited annually by boxing enthusiasts from all over the world.

From all that I have recorded about the written history of Boxing – and this is far from being complete – it can be readily accepted that the Fight Game has not been neglected by authors and writers, in fact, the New York Public Library in 1948 published a 28-page Bibliography of Boxing, a chronological check list of books in English published before 1900, compiled by Paul Magriel, that gave 120 specific items.

The coming of the camera brought Boxing even more into public notice. The saloon bars soon had pictures of prominent fighters adorning their walls; they could be bought in sport shops, and albums were produced, one of the most notable being published by Billy Edwards, former lightweight champion, in 1894 entitled: *The Portrait Gallery of Pugilists of England America and Australia*. It contained 89 photographs, $14\frac{1}{4}$in by 11in, plus six other pages devoted to punches, moves and ringcraft demonstrated by Young Griffo, a renowned featherweight, and his spar-mate, Walter Campbell. Sporting papers were quick to seize on this new selling line and the *Police Gazette* advertised boxers' photographs in series, as did *Health & Strength* and *Boxing*, and I revived the idea when becoming Editor of *Boxing News*. Also, in the days of Cigarette Cards, many tobacco firms issued series of boxers' pictures.

Of course, the invention of the moving-picture camera further enhanced Boxing's public image. First in the field was Thomas Edison, who was responsible for the gramophone and telephone. In 1894 he came up with his Kinetoscope which he claimed could take forty pictures a minute. He tried this out in his laboratories at Llewellyn in New Jersey with a studio bout between James J. Corbett, the reigning world heavyweight champion, and Peter Courtney, the exhibition ending in a flourish with the latter carefully taking the full count.

Edison's moving-pictures

In 1896 Edison got in touch with Dan Stuart, an enterprising carnival promoter, and arranged with him to film a contest between Bob Fitzsimmons and Peter Maher which was advertised as for the world's heavyweight championship, Corbett having announced his retirement. Unfortunately no one acquainted the boxers of the fact that moving-pictures of their fight were to be taken and shown all over the world, but Fitzsimmons got to hear of it and demanded extra payment. This was refused and 'Fitz' got his revenge by knocking out his opponent early in the first round, before the camera-men had time to start winding their handle.

A year later, when Corbett came back to defend his title against Fitzsimmons, the boxers had a share in the film rights, their contest going on record as being the first ever to be thrown on to a screen. It was shown at the Aquarium in London later in the same year. In 1908, a few months before he became champion, Jack Johnson visited Plymouth where he stopped Ben Taylor, known as The Woolwich Infant, in eight rounds. A film was made of this contest, believed to be the first in England. After that almost every fight of importance in all parts of the world was filmed and circulated among the increasing number of cinemas. The first 'sound' film of a contest was on the occasion of the fight for the vacant world heavyweight title between Max Schmeling and Jack Sharkey at Madison Square Garden, New York, on June 12, 1930, when the German became the first man in boxing history to win the championship on a foul.

The radio was the next stage in publicising Boxing. It was first used in America in 1919 at Toledo in Ohio when Jack Dempsey took the heavyweight title from Jess Willard, the result being telegraphed from the ringside. Two years later, a radio enthusiast, Andrew White, cashed in on the Million Dollar Gate championship fight between Dempsey and Carpentier. Although the show was a sell-out with 90,000 spectators, he thought it might be possible to bring the fight to the ears of countless more fans by means of a broadcast commentary. Getting the permission of the promoter, White sold his idea to theatre-owners throughout the United States, who were able to offer audiences a round-by-round account of the contest as it was actually taking place.

Then came a big snag in White's plans. He discovered that the radio equipment he intended to use was the property of the U.S. Navy. He was forbidden to take it to the big arena in Jersey City and it looked as though the project would fall through. He was not the type of man to take 'no' for an answer, however. He went right to the top in an effort to get the necessary permission and finally encountered a naval officer who was prepared to accept responsibility for the loan of the apparatus. White tested out the transmission on a minor contest to the main event, found it working effectively, then proceeded to tell his listeners how the gallant Frenchman tried hard to beat his tougher and stronger rival until put down and out in round four. This was the start of big fight broadcasting, thanks to the pertinacity of one man and the vision of another, the man of foresight being none other than Franklin Delano Roosevelt, later to become President of the United States.

First round K.O.

Jack Dempsey made a very brief radio telephone broadcast of the contest between Carpentier and Ted (Kid) Lewis at Olympia, London in 1922, it being all over in the first round and it was not until 1926 that the first real radio broadcast of a contest took place, this being the British featherweight championship bout between Johnny Curley and Harry Corbett at the National Sporting Club. This was the first time ringside chatter and the sounds of the fighting could be heard by the outside world, including a speech from the ring by comedian George Graves on behalf of the Boxers' Benevolent Fund which yielded the handsome amount of £551 in less than ten minutes. The following year came the first complete running commentary in England when Teddy Baldock met Willie Smith at the Albert Hall.

If Britain lagged behind America in the use of radio for Boxing, she was first to utilise television. At Broad-

The Computer Fight

In August 1968 the retired undefeated heavyweight champion of the world, Rocky Marciano, sparred 70 rounds with Muhammad Ali (Cassius Clay,) deposed heavyweight champion of the world for a film which was afterwards computerised for cinema screening in January 1970. No one would know who was the winner until it was shown and Marciano never knew as he was killed in an air crash a month later. It is believed that two endings to the film were made, one showing Marciano as the winner and the other with Clay victorious.

THE MEDIA

casting House on August 22, 1933, Archie Sexton and Lauri Raiteri, two London middleweights, boxed a six rounds exhibition bout before the TV cameras, yet it was not until April 4, 1938 that a contest was shown on closed circuit television, this being a match at Harringay Arena in which Len Harvey outpointed Jock McAvoy for the British light-heavyweight crown. The first fight televised on to London theatre screens and seen by the general public, was the famous British light-weight title bout on February 23, 1939 between Eric Boon and Arthur Danahar, also at Harringay.

The first important fight to be seen 'live' on a television screen in America was that between Max Baer and Lou Nova, in the Yankee Stadium, New York, on June 1st, 1939, but the first match televised on to theatre screens in New York – a middleweight championship fight between Billy Soose and Ken Overlin – was not until May 9, 1941. The first bout televised in colour took place at Madison Square Garden on March 26, 1954 between Gustav Scholz (Germany) and Al Andrews (U.S.A.), and the first title bout in colour came from the same arena on December 10, 1965 and was between Emile Griffith and Manuel Gonzales for the welterweight championship of the world.

Of course, the televising of big fights has developed into a world-wide business since those pioneer days and brought Fight Game audiences that must be assessed in millions. It has also taken the Richest Prize in Sport – the world heavyweight championship – to such remote places as Kinshasa in Zaire, when Ali regained the title by defeating George Foreman; at Kingston, Jamaica, (Foreman v. Frazier); Tokyo, Japan (Foreman v. Roman); Caracas, Venezuela (Foreman v. Norton); Kuala Lumpur (Ali v. Bugner) and Manila in the Philippines (Ali v. Frazier).

Today the boxing reporter has three fields in which to use his talents, whereas up to the time of radio and television it was confined to the simple, but exciting task of going to the arena equipped with pencil and notebook, or a small portable typewriter on which to record the exchanges by touch whilst watching the progress of a contest. If he was working for a daily paper the ring-side scribe was probably equipped with a telephone and during the interval between the rounds would dictate his

version of the previous round to an office telephonist. In the days before the installing of ringside telephones, it was a mad rush from the ringside after a big fight to get to the nearest telephone booth and rival reporters would get up to all manner of tricks to gain first use and so get their story into an edition that was standing ready to receive it.

I knew one man who screwed up the door of a phone box inside an arena and, being the only man in the place with a screwdriver, was able to scoop the result. Another had a confederate standing in the box from the start of the contest, ready to hand over as soon as the main bout came to an end. My own device for phone monopoly was to hang an 'Out of Order' card on the door handle and this was used successfully on a number of occasions. For the Don Cockell v. Harry Matthews contest at the White City in 1954, I telephoned to the London office of a Seattle news-paper after each round, my report being relayed by telephone during the following session, so that they had the full story round by round and the result in Matthews' home-town within a minute of it being over.

When I was working for a weekly publication, I equipped myself with a thick pad of large-sized paper and three or four finely-sharpened pencils. I was thus able to record all that was happening above me in the ring, including the important punches, any significant incidents, especially knock-downs. I did not look at my scribblings until the round had ended and even then it was necessary to keep an observant eye on what was going on in the corners in case a stoppage was impending or to see if either of the men were showing signs of wear and tear.

The major tournaments usually took place on a Tuesday evening, and we went to press the following morning. It was therefore necessary to write-up the notes during any supporting bout that might follow, include all the results and data, then wait until the very end of the show before driving to the printer to deliver my 'copy'. If writing for the morning sports edition of a daily paper, it was necessary to go from the arena overnight to deliver my report or get up early, around 6 30 a.m. and phone it in to a waiting telephonist.

It was all good, hard but rewarding work, from the moment one entered the boxing hall until the written account of the evening's happenings was safe in the hands of the compositor. To me

there was also the subsequent joy of reading my 'story' or better still, to be sitting beside someone in a public transport the following day and glance at them reading what I had written the night before in the unparalleled atmosphere that the boxing arena provides.

The reporter using a radio has no need to take notes, but he must be capable of producing a non-stop flow of description, getting a respite in the intervals between the rounds when he has someone beside him to take over and summarise the previous session and give an opinion on the way the fight is going. The commentator becomes an expert in unceasing chatter, even when there is a lull in the exchanges, when one man is endeavouring to entice his opponent into a false move. There must be no pauses and sitting beside a radio man sometimes I have often listened to his sustained eloquence and wondered if he and I were at the same fight.

The television commentator does not need to 'fill in', except during the intervals between rounds. He, too, must keep up a flow of conversation, explaining the tactics that are being employed, the damaging effect of punches and to add to what the viewer might not be observing. Before and during the contest he gives the background story of the two men engaged and generally maintains the interest, even to the extent of keeping his personal score card, the totals of which he declares from time to time. This, too, is a practice that between-the-rounds radio commentators also employ to maintain the atmosphere created by the actual spectators.

But whatever means are employed to entrance the listener or viewer, such as the use of glamour girls to carry the number cards, the singing of national anthems, the fanfares that precede the entry of the gladiators; the real and intense atmosphere of the fight arena, the traditions and the ritual, can only be felt by the actual spectator, who can give full tongue to his feelings and does so by right of having paid for admission.

I have sat in the topmost seat of the Albert Hall, the farthest away spot at the White City; spent an entire evening in a dressing-room and had my nose on the edge of the canvas countless times, all in the course of a life-time journalistic connection with the ring, and there is no substitute for the real thing.

120

April 4, 1938. Scene before the first contest to be shown on closed circuit television between Len Harvey and Jock McAvoy at Harringay.

February 23, 1939. The first fight to be televised on to London theatre screens was between Eric Boon (*right*) and Arthur Danahar at Harringay. The referee on that occasion was Barrington Dalby.

THE MEDIA
Space Age Boxing

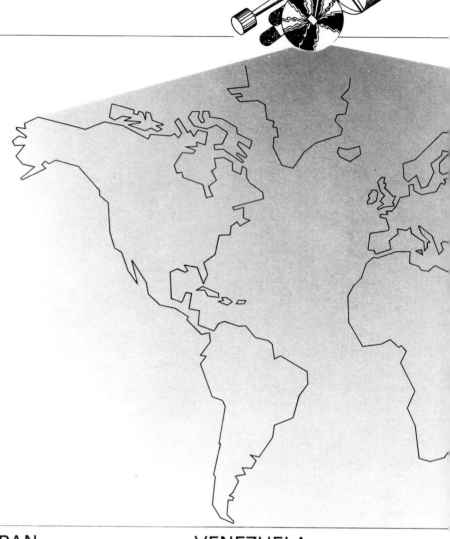

Boxing as a public spectacle has undergone amazing changes since the days of the Prize Ring when the onlookers stood around a turfed square or watched from any vantage point that might be available. With the coming of gloves the popularity of the sport increased and its exhibition became more permissive; it transferred to the small clubs, then the large arenas, indoors and out, with attendances becoming larger until the Million Dollar Gate was reached. But even this era was surpassed when, in their time, other mediums were found for bringing the action to the fight fan, until it has resulted in armchair watching in almost every home in the world.

At first accounts of great fights were relayed by word of mouth, followed by the printed broadsheets, then newspapers and with the coming of the camera, photographs, moving pictures, silent and sound; radio; next television, black and white, then colour, until finally televising by satellite to every part of the universe; bringing the viewers of fist fighting from a handful of spectators to hundreds, thousands and on to millions of fans.

JAMAICA

Foreman v Frazier
Kingston – 22.1.73

JAPAN

Foreman v Roman
Tokyo – 1.9.73

VENEZUELA

Foreman v Norton
Caracas – 26.3.74

Ali v Foreman	$5 million
Ali v Frazier	$6 million approx
Ali v Bugner	$2½ million

ZAIRE

Ali v Foreman
Kinshasa – 30.10.74

MALAYA

Ali v Bugner
Kuala Lumpur – 1.7.75

PHILIPPINES

Ali v Frazier
Manila – 1.10.75

CHRONOLOGY

1681 First known report of a Prize Ring contest – *Protestant Mercury*.

1719 James Fig or (Figg). First recognised Champion of England.

1723 Opening of The Ring in Hyde Park by order of King George I.

1740 First known book of Boxing – *A Treatise of the Useful Art of Self Defence* by Captain John Godfrey.

1743 John (Jack) Broughton drew up first Rules of Boxing and introduced the mufflers (gloves).

1811 *Pancratia: A History of Pugilism* by J.B. published by George Smeeton.

1812 *Boxiana: Sketches of Antient & Modern Pugilism* by George Smeeton.

1814 Formation of Pugilistic Club at Thatched House Tavern, London. Lord Byron spars with Gentleman John Jackson.

1818 *Boxiana* by Pierce Egan.

1820 John Jackson ordered to enlist band of Prize Ring boxers to keep order at Westminster Abbey on the occasion of the Coronation of King George IV.

1822 *Bell's Life in London* first published.

1824 First grandstand erected for a Prize Fight. Tom Spring v. Jack Langan, Worcester Racecourse, England.

1838 British Pugilists' Protection Association formed and London Prize Ring Rules or New Rules of Prize Fighting introduced.

1841 *Fistiana or The Oracle of the Ring*, by Frank Lewis Dowling.

1859 *Sporting Life* first published. Revised Prize Ring Rules introduced.

1860 First acclaimed International Prize Ring contest between Tom Sayers (British Champion) and John Camel Heenan (America) at Farnborough, Hampshire, England.

1863 Birth of Bob Fitzsimmons at Helston, Cornwall. First man to win three world titles. Middle 1891, Heavy 1897, Light-Heavy 1903.

1865 Marquess of Queensberry Rules introduced.

1866 Amateur Boxing Club (forerunner of Amateur Boxing Association) founded by John Chambers.

1873 Richard Kyle Fox first published the New York *Police Gazette*.

1880 *Pugilistica: The History of British Boxing*, by Henry Downes Miles. 3 volumes.

1882 First Madison Square Garden built in New York.

1889 Last heavyweight championship contest under Prize Ring Rules. John L. Sullivan (America) v. Jake Kilrain (Ireland) at Richburg, Miss. U.S.A.

1890 First world title fight with gloves in England. George Dixon (Canada) v. Nunc Wallace (England) at Pelican Club, London. Bantamweight. Madison Square Garden, New York rebuilt.

1891 Opening of National Sporting Club at King's Theatre, Covent Garden, London.

1892 First heavyweight championship contest under Marquess of Queensberry Rules. John L. Sullivan v. James J. Corbett at New Orleans, Louisiana, U.S.A.

1893 Longest bare-knuckle battle. Andy Bowen v. Jack Burke. 110 rounds, 7hrs. 19mins. at New Orleans, Louisiana, U.S.A.

1894 First boxing film. Exhibition match between James J. Corbett and Peter Courtney at Orange, New Jersey, U.S.A. 6 rounds. *Mirror of Life*, London weekly first published.

1897 First film ever made for public showing. Bob Fitzsimmons v. James J. Corbett at Carson City, Nevada, U.S.A. Heavyweight Championship of the World.

1899 'Wonderland' Boxing Arena opened in London's East End.

1902 Gum Shields invented by Jack Marks, London. First used by Ted (Kid) Lewis, multiple British champion and world welterweight titleholder.

1904 Boxing included in Olympic Games at St. Louis, Miss., U.S.A.

1905 Start of Boxing in France.

1907 Opening of the Cosmopolitan Club at Plymouth, England (The Old Cosmo).

1908 First World Heavyweight title fight to take place in Ireland. Tommy Burns (Canada) v. Jem Roche (Ireland) at Dublin. First world heavyweight title fight in Australia Rushcutter's Bay, Sydney. Tommy Burns (Canada) v. Jack Johnson (America). Promoter: Hugh D. McIntosh.

1909 Standardisation of eight weight divisions by National Sporting Club, London and introduction of the Lord Lonsdale Belts. *Boxing* first published.

1910 First use of 'Olympia', London, for Boxing Tournaments. Bill Lang (Australia) v. Jack Burns (America). Promoter: Hugh D. McIntosh. Boxing taken up in Germany.

1911 Original Liverpool Stadium opened for Boxing. 'Premierland' in London's East End opened. Frawley Law forbidding referees to render decisions operates in New York, U.S.A. Start of the No-Decision Bout era.

1914 Tom Andrews published his *Ring Battles of the Century* at Milwaukee, Winconsin, U.S.A.

1918 Jimmy Wilde received bag of diamonds valued at £2,000 after beating Joe Conn at Stamford Bridge, London. First use of Royal Albert Hall for Boxing. Inter-Allied King's Trophy tournament for servicemen. Formation of British Boxing Board of Control.

1919 First professional tournament at Royal Albert Hall, London. Ted (Kid) Lewis v. Matt Wells. Boxing Day.

1920 Walker Law introduced into New York, restored right of referees to render decisions. Named after Mayor Jimmy Walker who backed the bill. International Boxing Union formed in Europe, controlling World and European championships.

1921 First Million Dollar Gate. Jack Dempsey v. Georges Carpentier World's heavyweight championship at Boyles' 30 Acres, New Jersey, U.S.A. Attendance 80,183. Takings 1,789,238 dollars. Promoter: Tex Rickard. First radio broadcast of a boxing match.

1922 Nat Fleischer starts *The Ring*, monthly magazine, in New York.

1924 Wembley Stadium first used for boxing tournament. Jack Bloomfield v. Tom Gibbons. Promoter: J. Arnold Wilson.

1925 Tex Rickard builds new Madison Square Garden, New York.

1926 First full-length radio commentary of a championship contest. National Sporting Club. British featherweight championship. Johnny Curley v. Harry Corbett. First Golden Gloves (amateur) tournament in Chicago, Ill., U.S.A.

1927 Formation of the National Boxing Association in America. Battle of the Long Count. Gene Tunney v. Jack Dempsey for the world's heavyweight championship at Soldiers' Field, Chicago. Tunney down for 14 seconds. Referee: Dave Barry. Promoter: Tex Rickard. Tunney's purse 990,445 dollars.

1929 Re-constitution of British Boxing Board of Control.

1930 First German boxer to win World's Heavyweight title. Max Schmeling beat Jack Sharkey in New York.

1933 White City Stadium. London first used for boxing tournament. Jack Petersen v. Jack Doyle for British heavyweight title. Promoter: Jeff Dickson. Primo Carnera became first Italian to win Heavyweight Championship of the World.

1934 Wembley Pool & Sports Arena first used for boxing tournament, Len Harvey v. Walter Neusel. Promoter: Arthur Elvin.

1936 Harringay Arena first used for boxing tournament. Ben Foord (South Africa) v. Walter Neusel (Germany). Promoter: Sydney Hulls.

1937 First world championship fight in Scotland. Benny Lynch v. Peter Kane for flyweight title. Promoter: George Dingley, Glasgow.

1938 Henry Armstrong, born at Columbus, Miss. became first boxer ever to hold three world titles at one and the same time, i.e. Feather – 29.2.37, Welter – 31.5.38 and Light – 17.8.38. He also fought a draw for middleweight title. First contest ever to be televised. Len Harvey v. Jock McAvoy at Harringay Arena.

1939 First contest to be televised on closed circuit to theatre screens. Eric Boon v. Arthur Danahar for British lightweight title.

1940 *Boxing* renamed *Boxing News*.

1942 Willie Pep (William Guiglermo Papaleo) born at Middletown, Conn., U.S.A. became youngest boxer to win a world title in 40 years. He achieved this at the age of 20 years and 62 days and was unbeaten in 54 contests. Featherweight.

1945 Formation of European Boxing Union to control European Boxing Championships.

1949 Joe Louis (Joseph Louis Barrow), born Lafayette, Alabama, U.S.A. retired unbeaten as Heavyweight Champion of the World after record 25 defences of his title.

1951 Jersey Joe Walcott (Arnold Raymond Cream) born at Merchantville, New Jersey, U.S.A. became oldest boxer at 37½ years of age to win World's Heavyweight Title.

1953 First fight filmed in three dimensions, Rocky Marciano v. Jersey Joe Walcott. Heavyweight Championship of the World.

1956 Rocky Marciano (Rocco Francis Marchegiano) born at Brockton, Mass., U.S.A., retired undefeated for World's Heavyweight title after 49 contests and six successful title defences. Died in air crash 1969.

1958 Sugar Ray Robinson (Walker Smith) became first man ever to win Middleweight Championship of the World five times. Born at Detroit, Michigan, U.S.A. Floyd Patterson, born at Waco, North Carolina, U.S.A. became the youngest ever boxer to win the Heavyweight Championship of the World at 21 years and 10 months, at Chicago, Illinois, U.S.A.

1959 Ingemar Johansson became the first Swedish-born boxer to win the Heavyweight Championship of the World at New York, U.S.A.

1960 Floyd Patterson became first man to twice win World Heavyweight title, New York, U.S.A.

1963 World Boxing Council set up to control world championship contests and proceeded to make its own titleholders.

1964 Cassius Marcellus Clay, born Louisville, Kentucky, U.S.A., changed his name to Muhammad Ali and adopted the Muslim Faith after winning the World's Heavyweight title from Sonny Liston at Miami Beach, Florida, U.S.A.

1965 Former National Boxing Association became World Boxing Association in opposition to W.B.C.

1967 Muhammad Ali forfeited championship by refusal to accept service in the U.S. Armed Forces after nine successful title defences. Henry Cooper, born Bellingham, England. First man to win outright three Lord Lonsdale Belts.

1968 Computerised film made of contest between Rocky Marciano and Muhammad Ali in colour. Two versions with each man made the winner.

1974 Muhammad Ali became second man to twice win World's Heavyweight Championship, Kinshasa, Zaire.

1978 Leon Spinks was stripped of the World Heavyweight Title by default which he won from Muhammed Ali in Las Vegas and Ken Norton was declared World Heavyweight Champion by the World Boxing Council without a fight.

Index

Bold figures denote illustration

A

	Page No.
Abbott, Bill	13
Abingdon Baird, Squire	112
Agnello, Joe	110
Ahlqvist, Eddie	100
Allen, Tom	14
Ambers, Lou	36, **91**
Andrews, Al	120
Andrews, T. S.	117, 125
Apostoli, Fred	101
Archibald, Joey	78
Arguello, Alexis	105
Armstrong, Henry (Jackson, Henry)	**35**, 35, 93, **125**
Attell, Abe	36, 100

B

	Page No.
Baer, Max	33, 76, 101, 111, 120
Bailey, L. N. (Bill)	117
Baldock, Teddy	101, 118
Ballarati, Giuseppe	117
Barrett, Mike	**99**, 100
Barrington, Dalby	**121**
Barry, Dave	125
Battling Siki, (Phal, Louis)	**34**, 34
Becket, Joe	100, 103
Belcher, Jem	12
Belcher, Tom	12
Bell, John	116
Benaim, Gilbert	103
Bendigo, William (Thompson, William)	13
Benvenuti, Nino	24, 35
Berg, Jack (Kid)	36
Berks, Joe	12
Berry, Brothers	117
Best, Johnny	**100**, 100
Bettinson, Arthur	112
Blake, George	78
Bloomfield, Jack	103, 125
Boggis, Arthur	43
Boon, Eric	101, 103, 107, 111, 120, **121**, 125
Botein, Justice Bernard	110
Bowen, Andy	124
Braddock, James J.	33, 97
Bradley, Frank	117
Brady, William A.	**51**, 51
Breyer, Victor	117
Brighton, Bill (Phelps, Bill)	13
Britton, Jack	35, 51, 111
Broadribb, Ted	**50**, 50, 78, 97
Broughton, John	31, 86, 114, 124
Brown, Alphonse Theo	29, **37**, 37
Brown, Jackie	37
Brusa, Amilca,	35
Bugner, Joe	**120**
Burke, James	13, 124, 125
Burns, Tommy	16, 29, 32, 102, 125
Burruni, Salvatore	78
Buxton, Alex	18
Buxton, Allan	18
Buxton, Joe	18
Buxton, Laurie	18

Byrne, Simon	13
Byron, Lord	12, 124

C

	Page No.
Callahan, Mushy	105
Campbell, Walter	118
Canto, Miqual	105
Cannon, Tom	13
Canzoneri, Tony	36, 104
Captain Cook	8
Carnera, Primo	**16**, 16, 17, 33, 78, 111, 113, 125
Carpentier, Georges	17, **21**, 34, 50, 92, 100, 101, 103, 108, **110**, 110, 111, 118, 125
Castillo, Chuchu	37
Castillo, Freddie	105
Caunt, Big Ben	13
Cavilli, Nick	81
Cerdan, Marcel	17, **21**, 35
Cervantes, Antonio	105
Chambers, John Graham	16, 124
Chandler, Tom	17
Charles, Ezzard	78
Charnley, Dave	102
Chavez, Simon	78
Christenberry, Bob	110
Clarence, The Duke of	12
Clay, Cassius — see Muhammad Ali	
Coburn, Joe	14
Cochran, Charles B.	**100**, 100, 103
Cockell, Don	33, 103, 120
Coffroth, James J.	100
Cohen, Robert	17, 37, 78
Conn, Joe	125
Cook, George	**110**, 110
Cooper, George	12
Cooper, Henry	18, 30, **73**, 81, **93**, 102, 107, 112, 125
Cooper, Jim	18
Corbett, Dick (Coleman)	18, 50
Corbett, Harry (Coleman)	18, 50, 118, 125
Corbett, James, J. (Gentleman Jim)	16, 17, 31, 32, 51, 100, 107, 113, 118, 124, 125
Corbett I, Young — see Green, George	
Corbett II, Young — see Rothwell, William	
Corbett III, Young — see Giordano, Ralph Capabianca	
Corri, Eugene	80, 86, 110
Courtney, Peter	118, 124
Crawley, Peter	13
Cribb, Tom	12, **13**, 14, 116
Criqui, Eugene	17
Cumberland, The Duke of	114
Cunningham, Bob	15
Curley, Johnny	118, 125
Curvis, Brian	18
Curvis, Cliff	18

D

	Page No.
Dade Harold	37
D'Agata, Mario	37
D'Amato, Gus	**51**, 51
Danahar, Arthur	101, 120, **121**, 125
Darewski, Max	107
Davis, Al (Bummy)	111
Delaney, Jack	68
Dempsey, Jack	17, 20, 21, **32**, 32, 33, 34, 42, 50, 68, 76, 78, **90**, **92**, 102, 103, 108, 113, 118, 125
Descamps, Francois	**50**, 50, 110
Dickson, Jeff	33, **100**, 100, 103, 125
Dingley, George	125

Dixie, Kid (Brown, Aaron)	109
Dixon, George	36, 124
Donmall, Charles	106
Donnelly, Dan	12
Donovan, Arthur	76
Douglas, 'Pickles' C. F.	58
Downes, Terry	26
Doyle, Jack	51, 101, 125
Driscoll, Jim	36, **113**, 113
Duff, Mickey	**99**
Duffy, Paddy	17
Dundee, Angelo	81
Dundee, Joe	105
Dundee, Johnny	111
Duran, Roberto	105

E

	Page No.
Eagan, Eddie	26
Edinburgh, The Duke of	103
Edison, Thomas	118
Edwards, Billy	118
Egan, Pierce	114, 116, **118**, 124
Elliot, Gilbert C.	107
Ellis, Jimmy	106
Elvin, Arthur	**101**, 101, 125
Erne, Frank	58
Ertle, Harry	109
Escobar, Sixto	78
Espada, Gustavo	105

F

	Page No.
Famechon, Alfred	18
Famechon, Andre	18
Famechon, Arsenne	18
Famechon, Emile	18
Famechon, Johnny	18
Famechon, Ray	18
Farr, Tommy	20, 33, 50, 97, 101
Fig (or Figg) James	9, 114, 124
Finnegan, Chris	18
Finnegan, Kevin	18
Firpo, Luis Angel	32
Fitzsimmons, Bob	14, 16, 18, 20, **21**, 31, 32, 42, 51, 100, 113, 116, 118, 124
Fleischer, Nat	28, 78, 107, **118**, 125
Fleming, John	112
Flowers, Tiger	68
Foord, Ben	33, 125
Foreman, George	24, **95**, 102, 120, **122**, 123
Fox, Billy	111
Fox, Richard Kyle	107, 116, 124
Frazier, Joe	24, **25**, **93**, 102, 106, 120, **122**, 123
Frazier, Marvis	**25**
Frush, Danny	102

G

	Page No.
Gains, Larry	101, 102
Galindez, Victor	105
Gans, Joe	35, 46, 58, 102, 111
Garcia, Ceferino	78
Gattellari, Rocky	78
Gazo, Eddie	105
Genaro, Frankie	24, 104
George I, King	124
George IV, Prince of Wales	111, 124
Giardello, Joey	110
Gibbons, Tommy	103, 125
Giordano, Ralph Capabianca	21
Godfrey, Captain John	114, 124
Goldstein, Ruby	81, 109, 110
Gomez Wilfredo	105
Gonzales, Manuel	120

Goss, Joe 14
Gottert and Gretzschel 103
Graham, Billy 110
Graham, Bushy 104
Graves, George 118
Graziano, Rocky 112
Greb, Harry, **34**, 34, 111
Green, George 21
Gregson, Bob 12
Griffith, Emile **90**, 120
Griffo, Young 118
Gully, John 12
Gushiken, Yoko 105

H
                                Page No.
Hampston, Len 81
Harvey, Len 20, **21**, 34, 42, 51,
                                59, 101, 109,
                                120, **121**, 125
Haynes, Leroy 113
Hecht, Gerhard **108**, 109
Heenan, John, C. 13, **14**, 107,
                                116, 124
Heeney, Tom 76
Henning, Fred 116
Hogarth, William 9
Holland, Danny **73**
Hood, Jack 38, 50
Hook, Walter 110
Hulls, Sydney 97, **101**, 101,
                                125
Humez, Charles 17
Humphreys, Richard **12**, 114
Hurst, Sam 14
Hyer, Jacob 16, 17
Hyer, Tom 16

J
                                Page No.
Jackson, John 124
Jackson, Peter 14, 113
Jacobs, Harry 101
Jacobs, Joe **51**, 51
Jacobs, Mike 17, 33, 97, **101**,
                                101, 102, 113
Jarvis, Ernie 102
Jefferies, Jim
    (James Jackson) 32, 51
Jenkins, Lew 42
Johansson, Ingemar **16**, 16, 33, 51,
                                92, 100, 125
Johnson, Harold 18
Johnson, Jack 32, 34, **90**, 102,
                                118, 125
Johnson, Phil 18
Johnston, Jimmy **51**, 51

K
                                Page No.
Kahut, Joe 78
Kane, Peter 37, 100, 125
Kearns, Jack 'Doc' **50**, 50
Keating, John 17
Kelly, Billy 18
Kelly, Jim (Spider) 18
Kelly, John 37
Kelly, Tommy 17
Ketchel, Stanley
    (Kiecal, Stanislaus) 21, 34, 100
Kilrain, Jake (Owens, Harry) 16, 21, 32, 124
King, Don **95**, 102
King, Tom 14
Knorzer, Willy 103

L
                                Page No.
Lake, Bugler Harry 103
La Motta, Jake 35, 111
Lang, Bill 125
Langan, Jack 13, 124
Lastra, Cecilio 105
Layne, Rex 78
Ledoux, Charles 17, 103,
                                113, 113

Lee, Glen 78
Leonard, Benny
    (Liener, Benjamin) **36**, 36
Lesnevich, Gus 34, 78, 105
Levene, Harry **102**, 102, 103
Levine, Rene 103
Lewis, John Henry 101
Lewis, Ted (Kid)
    (Mendeloff, Gershon) 35, 51, 103
                                107, 110, 111,
                                118, 125
Lewis, Willie 109
Liston, Sonny 33, 80, **93**, 125
London, Brian 18
London, Jack 18, 103
Longford, Lord 13
Lonsdale, The 5th Earl of **28**, 106, 107
Lopez, Danny 105
Loughran, Tommy 105, 111
Louis, Joe
    (Barrow, Joseph Louis) 17, **20**, 20, **33**, 33,
                                42, 50, 97, 101,
                                102, 105, **109**,
                                109, 110,
                                112, 125
Lowther, Lord 12
Lugan, Jorge 105
Lynch, Benny 20, **37**, 37, 81,
                                101, 125
Lynch, Charley 17

M
                                Page No.
Mace, Jem 14, 15, 16
Magri, Charlie **25**
Magriel, Paul 118
Maher, Peter 118
Mallin, Fred 26
Mallin, Harry 26
Mancini, Alf 38
Mancini, Denny **46**
Mandell, Sammy 104
Marchant, Albert 18
Marchant, Billy 18
Marchant, Jack 18
Marchant, Mark 18
Marchant, Matthew 18
Marchant, Teddy 18
Marciano, Rocky
    (Marchegiano, Rocco) **33**, 33, 42, 102,
                                112, **119**, 125
Marks, Jack 125
Marino, Dado **91**
Mason, Harry 101
Matthews, Harry 120
Mattoli, Rocky 105
Maxim, Joey 34, 50
McAuliffe, Jack 17
McAvoy, Jock
    (Bamford, Joseph) 21, 59, 101, 109,
                                120, **121**, 125
McCoy, Kid 29, 30
McGovern, Terry
    (John Terence) 20, **36**, 36, 111
McGovern, Tommy 111
McIntosh, Hugh D. **102**, 102, 125
McLarnin, Jimmy 35
McMoneghan, John 17
McTigue, Mike 34, 109
Mendoza, Daniel **12**, 12, 114
Mildenberger, Karl 59
Miles, Henry Downes 114, 124
Miller, Ray 110
Miller, Walk 68
Milligan, Tommy 35, 80, 100, 101
Mills, Freddie 20, **34**, 34, 50,
                                103, 105, 112
Minter, Alan **55**, **61**,
Mitchell, Charlie Watson **15**, 15, 16, 17
Mobuto, President 102
Molyneaux, Tom 12, **13**, 14, 116
Monaghan, Rinty 37, 105
Monroe, Judge 110
Monson, Carlos 35
Montana, 'Small' 37, 101
Moore, Archie
    (Wright, Archibald Lee) 34, 111

Moore, Roy 110
Moore, Ted 102
Moran, Frank 103
Moran, Owen 100
Morgan, Dan 51
Morgan, Ted 104
Muangsurin, Saensak 105
Muhammad Ali
    (Cassius Clay) **24**, 24, **34**, 34, 59,
                                78, 80, 81, **93**, **95**,
                                102, 104, 105,
                                112, **119**, 120,
                                123, 125
Murphy, Billy 17
Murray, John 117
Myers, Arthur 109

N
                                Page No.
Nelson, Oscar 'Battling' **35**, 35, 46,
                                100, 102
Neusel, Walter 33, 101, 125
Norris, Jim **102**, 102
Norton, Ken 93, 120, **122**, 125
Nova, Lou 120

O
                                Page No.
O'Gatty, Packey 110
Olivares, Ruben 37
Oliver, Tom 13
O'Rourke, Samuel 13
Ortiz, Manuel **37**, 37, 105
Overlin, Ken 120

P
                                Page No.
Painter, Ned 13
Palmer, Joe 109, 110
Palmer, Pedlar 36
Palmerston, Lord 14
Palomino, Carlos 105
Paret, Benny (Kid) **90**
Parlov, Mate 105
Paterson, Jackie **37**, 37
Patterson, Floyd 24, 33, 34,
                                51, **92**, 125
Pearce, Henry 12
Pep, Willie (Papaleo,
    William Guiglermo) **36**, 36, 105, 125
Perez, Pascual 24
Persson, Harry 34
Peterborough, The Earl of 114
Petersen, Jack 101, 109, 125
Powell, C. B. 110
Prince Regent, The 12

Q
                                Page No.
Queensberry, The Duke of 12
Queensberry, The 8th
    Marquess of **16**, 16, 86,
                                104, 124

R
                                Page No.
Raiteri, Laurie 120
Revie, Jimmy **46**
Richmond, Bill 12
Rickard, George (Tex) 17, 102,
                                103, 125
Ritchie, Willie 36, 86, 100
Roberts, Jack 109
Robinson, Sugar Ray
    (Smith, Walker) **20**, 20, 35, 42, 81,
                                91, 103, 105,
                                108, 109, 112,
                                125
Roche, Jem 125
Roderick, Ernie 100, 107
Roman, Joe 120, **122**
Roosevelt, Franklin Delano 118
Rose, Lionel 37

Rosner, Johnny — 37
Ross, Barney
 (Rosofsky, Barnet) — 20, **35**, 35, 36
Rothenburg, Walter — 103
Rothschild, Baron — 15
Rothwell, William — 21
Routis Andre — 104
Ryan, Paddy — 16, 32

S

	Page No.
Saddler, Sandy	**36**, 36, 105
Sands, Alfie	18
Sands, Clem	18
Sands, Dave	18
Sands, George	18
Sands, Ritchie	18
Sands, Russell	18
Sangchilli, Baltazar	37
Sanger, 'Lord' John	71
Sayers, Tom	13, **14**, 14, 107, 116, 124
Schmeling, Max	**16**, 16, 17, 20, 33, 51, 78, **92**, 97, 118, 125
Scholz, Gustav	120
Schulz, Wilfred	103
Scott, Phil	51, 101
Serrano, Samuel	105
Sexton, Archie	120
Sharkey, Jack (Zukauskas, Joseph Paul)	21, 33, **92**, 111, 118, 125
Shirai, Yoshio	**91**
Singer, Al	36
Singleton, Joey	107
Slavin, Frank	17, 112, 133
Smeeton, George	124
Smith, Billy (Livingstone, Murray)	17, 109
Smith, Jem	17, 112
Smith, Gunboat	**110**, 110
Smith, Jack	**110**, 110
Smith, Willie	118
Solomons, Jack	94, 102, **103**, 103, 117
Songkitrat, Chamrern	37, 78
Soo, Hwan Hong	105
Soose, Billy	120
Spinks, Leon	**93**, 105, 125
Spring, Tom	13, 124
Stribling, Young Bill	78, 109, 111
Stuart, Dan	118
Sullivan, Dan	51
Sullivan, Jack	18
Sullivan, John L.	**15**, 15, 16, 17, 32, 51, 107, 113, 124
Sullivan, Johnny	109
Sullivan, Mike	18
Swift, Owen	13

T

	Page No.
Tarleton, Nel	100
Taylor, Ben	118
Taylor, Charles Bud	104
Terrell, Ernie	106
Thil, Marcel	101
Thompson, Billy	111
Toweel, Frazer	18
Toweel, Jimmy	18
Toweel, Victor	18, 37
Toweel, Willie	18, 37, 102
Tunney, Gene	20, 32, 33, 34, 76, **90**, 103, 105, 112, 125
Turpin, Dick	18
Turpin, Jackie	18
Turpin, Randolph	18, 35, 81, **91**, 103, 112

U

	Page No.
Uzcudun, Paolino	17, 111

V

	Page No.
Valan, Harold	78
Valdes, Rodrigo	105
Vesey, Joe	112
Vienne, Theo	103
Villa, Pancho	37
Volante, Dom	100

W

	Page No.
Walcott, Jersey Joe	18, 33, 80, **109**, 110, 125
Wales, Prince of (later Edward VII)	16
Walker, Major Jimmy	16, 125
Walker, Micky (Walker Edward Patrick)	**35**, 35, 50, 80, 100, 105, 108
Wallace, Nunc	124
Waltham, Teddy	59, 78
Ward, Jem	13
Wells, Bombardier Billy	18, 108
Wells, Matt	125
Welsh, Freddie (Thomas Frederick, Hall)	21, **36**, 36, 86, 100, 112
West, George	102
White, Andrew	118
White, James	112
Wilde, Jimmy	18, 20, **37**, 37, 112, 125
Williams, Ike	105
Williams, Johnny	50
Willard, Jess	32, 33, 68, **90**, 118
Wilson, Arnold	**103**, 103, 125
Winstone, Howard	107
Wolgast, Ad	35
Woodcock, Bruce	34, 103

Y

	Page No.
York, The Duke of	12
Young, Zulu Kid	37

Z

	Page No.
Zale, Tony	35, 105
Zarate, Carlos	105
Zivic, Eddie	18
Zivic, Fritzie	18
Zivic, Jack	18
Zivic, Joe	18
Zivic, Pete	18

CREDITS AND ACKNOWLEDGEMENTS

Illustrations:
Bryan Austin/ Francoise Trainaud.

Photography:
Associated Press : 16/24/95/99/122.

Bryan Austin : Covers, 2/3/4/5/18/19/22/
23/29/38/39/40/41/43/44/45/46/47/48/
49/53/54/55/56/57/58/59/60/61/62/63/
69/70/71/76/77/80/87.

The Author's Library : 6/15/16/20/21/28/
32/33/34/35/36/37/50/51/73/89/90/91/
92/100/101/102/103/108/109/110/113/
119/121/122.

British Museum : 6.

Camera Press : 16.

The Mansell Collection : 9/10/11/13/14/
15/124.

Popperfoto : 8/12/25/92/93/122/123.

Sporting Press : 25/79.

Syndication International : 34.

Artwork:
David Laraman : 96/104/105/122/123.

The Author, the editor and the publishers
also acknowledge with gratitude the help
given to them by the following :
R. L. Clarke, General Secretary of the
British Boxing Board of Control, "Thomas
A'Beckett", Danny Holland, Dave Old,
Denny Mancini, London Weekend
Television, Jimmy Revie, The Norwood
Boy's Boxing Club.